Through Other Eyes

Developing Empathy and Multicultural Perspectives in the Social Studies

JOAN SKOLNICK

NANCY DULBERG

THEA MAESTRE

Pippin

Graphics: Gwynnd Maestre
Photo consultant: Bill Dane
Designed by John Zehethofer
Edited by Sean Stokes
Typeset by Heidy Lawrance Associates
Printed and bound in Canada by Friesens

Canadian Cataloguing in Publication Data

Dulberg, Nancy
  Through other eyes

(The Pippin teacher's library; 29)
Includes bibliographical references.
ISBN 0-88751-088-4

1. Social sciences — Study and teaching. 2. History — Study and
teaching. 3. Multicultural education. I. Maestre, Thea. II. Skolnick, Joan.
III. Title. IV. Series.

LB1584.D842 1998   300'.71   C98-932603-9

Credits
p. 30 *"My Precious Water, I Kiss You"*, by Parkpoom Poompana, Age 15,
Grand Prize —1996 *River of Words* Environmental Poetry and Art
Contest © 1996 International Rivers Network; p. 82 Shea, P.D., illustrated
by Anita Riggio, stitched by You Yang, *The Whispering Cloth: A Refugee's
Story*, Honesdale, Pennsylvania: Boyds Mills Press, 1995; p. 72 printed
with permission from Evans Brothers Limited Extract from: *One Day We
Had to Run!* by Sybella Wilkes. First published in 1994 by Evans
Brothers Limited, 2A Portman Mansions, Chiltern Street, London W1M
1LE, UK. Copyright © in text, photographs and children's paintings
Sybella Wilkes 1994; p. 131 Anita Shriver/Bancroft Human Relations
Club; permission to reproduce/adapt activities granted by: Valerie
Welsh, Matica Manuel, Anita Jones, Lisa Alba.

. . . .

DEDICATION

To: Alex, Elizabeth, Esther, Jesse,
Michael, Moses... and all the children

. . . .

ACKNOWLEDGMENTS

We gratefully acknowledge the following individuals who contributed to the evolution of our thinking and writing: Matt Downey, Bernice McCarthy, Paul Ammon, and Randy Reiter; our colleagues at Holy Names College, Saint Mary's College, the University of California, Berkeley, and the Teacher Education Collaborative Conversation Group. We are indebted to the Saint Mary's College of California Alumni Association for generously providing financial support for this project.

A special thanks to the following teachers: Lisa Alba, Anita Jones, Matica Manuel, and Valerie Welsh for their contributions to the activities "No Loyal Citizen," "Children at Work," and "Owls and Jobs"; to Lois Breault for introducing us to the Personal History Suitcase, and to Erica Hagen for information and resources about Cambodian refugee camps.

Our deepest gratitude goes to our families — our parents, children, grandchildren, and partners Bill, Randy, and Jose. Thank you.

. . . .

CONTENTS

PART ONE *Learning to Take Perspective*

CHAPTER ONE

VIEWING THE WORLD

THROUGH DIFFERENT EYES

INTRODUCTION: HABITS OF HEART AND MIND

> Being Black in my town makes me think people still judge others by their skin color. They are looking at me as if to say "Please don't take my purse." They don't know I have enough money in my pocket to buy them a new one.
>
> *Michael*

> I want everyone to know that Mexicans like me have the same dreams and hopes as people of other races. I care about my future, my life, my friends and my family.
>
> *Liz*

> My ancestors came from China and Japan. I have a lot of friends who are different and that makes us special in our own way. Sometimes it can be hard…. For example, everyone thinks I am so smart [but] my life has not been easy. They don't know my true story.
>
> *Leslie*[1]

These are the voices of our students. Their stories are with them as they face each other in the classroom, on the school yard and in the streets. What they make of their histories and the way they come together to solve problems and resolve conflicts will shape the future of us all.

Their stories reflect the extraordinary demographic and social changes that are transforming the daily reality of our lives. Nearly half of the school children in the United States are children of color. Forty percent of Canadians are people whose origins are neither British nor French. A fifth of U.S. children live

1

below the poverty line. Many of these children are part of what the United Nations calls "an unprecedented global phenomenon, a new age of migration in which 100 million people have left their homes and moved across borders to escape poverty, war, and oppression. Beneath the statistics lies an ethnically troubled world. Yet it is, in Maxine Greene's words, a "world lived in common", economically, environmentally, and technologically interdependent.[2]

As teachers, we can play a crucial role in helping our students to venture outside of their own experience — which is so compelling — in order to understand their classmates and their world. We can seek strategies to build empathy, inclusion and community in the classroom; to foster pride in heritage, respect for diversity and another's point of view; and ultimately to foster in students a willingness to challenge prejudice in themselves and others. These are the goals of multicultural and anti-bias/anti-racist curriculum approaches. We believe that social studies can and must have a central place in this endeavor.

If we believe students ought to develop empathy and to consider other points of view, then we need to systematically teach to these goals. This book provides a teaching model for the social studies, using a developmental pattern of questions and activities. It is designed to help students use historical evidence, respond to people in varied circumstances, to think about how the world might look through their eyes and be able to explain it. Students generate their own questions to research: How are you like me? What is your life like? What might you feel or think? How can I find out? Are there other people like you? How would I feel in your position? What would I do? The model develops habits of critical and multi-dimensional thinking that research indicates reduces prejudice and helps students act compassionately and responsibly in their world.

Historian Russell Freedman called history "the story of ourselves."[3] It is quintessentially about people, people who, like us, have needs and dreams, who work and have families and memories, who build communities, have conflicts, take actions, and come together to solve problems. Students need to see themselves in history. Because they need a personal bridge to the past and active, concrete ways of learning, we propel students into the human drama and dilemmas of history.

2

Premises about Learning and Historical Understanding

We base this book on several premises about how students learn and about the nature of historical understanding.

- Our first premise is that students learn through active engagement with their physical and social world. Students naturally grapple with social issues that are a part of their daily lives, and create their understanding of others and themselves from their interactions and observations. We can bring this natural, intrinsically motivating process into the social studies classroom by focusing on the human stories and conflicts of history. Such a process involves both thinking and feeling (cognition and affect). Students can use early "concrete" experiences to build personal understandings about society, history and human relations. By emphasizing peer interaction, links to literature, writing and the arts, we help students to actively inquire about the experience of others.

- Our second premise is that perspective-taking is key to historical understanding. Learning history is about learning to understand the people in the past, not only learning the chronology of history. The study of multiple perspectives ought to be a central guiding principle of the social studies curriculum. The ability to understand and describe the past through the eyes and experiences of the peoples who lived it is fundamental to the nature of historical thinking. One cannot understand why a historical event unfolded as it did, nor comprehend its legacy, if one is unable to explain how the situation looked to its varied participants. Thus, teaching students to inquire about the past and to uncover its multiple stories not only motivates them, it also fosters more authentic historical analysis.

- Finally, we believe that when students see people like themselves in the history they study, they are more likely to envision themselves as active agents empowered to move history forward. As history educator Linda Levstik put it, we prepare them "to act in the world based on their historical understanding."(4) Such a vision builds the thoughtful and socially responsible citizenry vital to a democratic society.

We all have a vital stake in developing students' ability to be empathic and to understand the perspectives of the other people who share their world. This ability to "walk in another's shoes" (**perspective-taking**) is fundamental to students' motivation to learn history and to the resolution of current social tensions that are rooted in history. These are the habits of mind and heart that we can foster in our classrooms.

The Teaching Model in "Through Other Eyes"

THE THINKING-FEELING SPIRAL

The **Thinking-Feeling Spiral** is the curriculum model we use throughout this book. The spiral consists of four major kinds of learning experiences: **making personal and concrete connections** to the topic; **inquiring and imagining** about someone else's life; **investigating content resources** to learn more about a group's experience; and **"acting as if"** one is actually in another's circumstances, making choices or solving problems. The Thinking-Feeling Spiral is described in detail in Chapter Two. We encourage you to use the models and strategies we provide to create Thinking-Feeling Spirals in your own curriculum context.

KEY SOCIAL STUDIES THEMES

In this book, we present a developmental sequence that moves students from their own experience to the experience of another, and from one individual's story to the story of many people (a collective history). The exemplar activities in Part Two focus on four key areas of history and social studies through which students may uncover and understand different perspectives: personal and family history, work, migration and conflict and change.

Personal/Family History Family relationships are a fundamental part of culture. Looking at their own family histories and those of their classmates helps students affirm their own heritage, and understand various peoples' dilemmas. Students also see how the accumulated decisions of people "like you and me" contributed to history.

Work Work is a critically important aspect of daily life and another basic dimension of culture. Social differences between groups are often evident in the kinds of work available to people and what they are paid for it. Because work has such a profound effect on our lives, learning about how different work situations shape people's lives and relationships is key to taking another's perspective.

4

Migration Our communities and classrooms reflect the movement of peoples within and across borders — people moving from one place to another, following the push of necessity and the pull of dreams. By studying migration stories, we help students explore why people move, what it's like to leave home and struggle to survive as an "outsider" in a new land, how people in the "receiving community" react and how they might help newcomers.

Conflict and Change Conflict by definition is a situation where different interests or values confront one another. Conflicts often powerfully reveal underlying differences hidden in our everyday lives. Studying conflict and the push for change heightens opportunities to understand diverse perspectives.

SIX KEY STRATEGIES FOR DEVELOPING EMPATHY AND PERSPECTIVE-TAKING

The exemplar activities given in Part Two of this book use six perspective-taking strategies: perspectives through personal and family history, through artifacts, through children's literature, through writing, through the arts, and through "experiencing" history. These six strategies are described in detail in Chapter Three. Using a developmental pattern of questioning with the six strategies we provide, you can help your students learn to take perspective and develop empathy.

Empathy and Perspective-Taking: What Are They?

The ability to put oneself in another's shoes involves both **affect** (feeling) and **cognition** (thinking). We think of empathy as the more affective component, and perspective-taking as the more cognitive. In empathizing, you feel *for* another by making a personal connection, reaching down inside yourself for that kernel of "like" experience that you have encountered. You may not know how it feels to be a refugee, but you may know what it feels like to be separated from family and friends. In taking another's perspective, you go beyond feelings. You seek to understand *why* the other person might think or act as he or she does and try to explain it from his or her point of view. Perspective-taking carries with it the power of explanation, so critical to historical understanding and to problem-solving. In history, understanding perspectives is a first step toward explaining human actions.[5]

Empathy is a goal in itself — we want our students to be empathetic towards others. Empathy, though, is also a motivator. When

5

students care, they develop a need to know, which drives their inquiry about what life is like for someone else. Eleven-year-olds looking at photos of children working in a mill or sweatshop in the nineteenth century might ask, "Why did the children have to work? Where were their parents? How did they go to school? Could they talk to their friends? How old are they? How long did they have to sit there?"

Empathy can also propel students to grapple with issues of fairness, a riveting issue for students in their own daily lives. They might ask: Is this person or group being treated fairly, the way I want to be treated? The question pushes students to try to explain what it's like for the other person, to search for information, gather data, to ask why, and to search for solutions that will make unfair things fair. Here are the eleven-year-olds again: "Why didn't someone *do* something about this [child labor]? Why didn't they arrest the bosses? What would I have done? Do children still work in sweatshops? What can we do to change this?" Thus, empathy and perspective-taking, feeling and thinking, work together. They are two parts of a process that lead to social and historical understanding.

Perspective-taking is quite different from voice-appropriation. No one can completely understand what it is like to "be" someone else, but in the process of trying to glimpse another's reality, we ask questions, we challenge our assumptions, and we develop a more empathetic stance toward other people who share our world. As teachers, we need to be sensitive to situations where aspects of perspective-taking may be inappropriate; for example, in the retelling of oral tales which only a culture's elders are permitted to tell, or where the situation is too complex or sensitive for perspective-taking activities.

LEARNING TO TAKE ANOTHER'S PERSPECTIVE

In children's early social behaviors, we already find seeds of empathy and perspective-taking. A preschooler, for example, may bring her own "cuddly" to comfort another child who has lost a toy. From early on, too, children worry about how they and other people are treated, about turn-taking and about aggression. They struggle with right and wrong, good and bad. In this process, they "construct morality out of daily life experiences," as educators Rheta DeVries and Betty Zan state in their book, *Moral Classrooms, Moral Children.* They are developing a sense of fairness and increasing their understandings of similarities and differences among people.[6]

Throughout the elementary years, students come to better

understand that each person has a unique perspective. They shift from egocentric thought (thinking exclusively about one's own experiences) to thinking about others ("decentering"). Every teacher has a favorite story about a student's egocentrism. One teacher recalled her conversation when she asked nine-year-old Matthew what birthday present he wanted to get his father. He replied, "a space station game." Matthew's response is typical of the egocentric thinking of younger students. He thought of what he wanted, and attributed that desire to his father. He was unable to differentiate his own birthday wish from his father's.

But students can and do make empathic connections to begin to build perspective. After reading a story written by a child in a shelter for the homeless, this eight-year-old wrote:

If I was the homeless girl living at the shelter I would feel sad because my friends are not with me. I can't even call them. Maybe I'd make a new friend at the shelter, but maybe he'd never come back after today. I think she didn't deserve to be homeless.

In real life, children build their understandings of the social world and of morality through daily interactions with peers and adults. Children try out different approaches and solutions to social dilemmas such as: What happens when I don't take turns? How does my friend react when I grab his toy? What does it feel like to be left out? What makes a rule fair? This natural social learning process, when reproduced in the classroom is the social studies equivalent of "hands-on" experimentation in math and science. When students participate in activities that cause them to bump up against social problems faced by real people, they have a chance to weigh choices and resolve dilemmas, mirroring the natural learning process in real life.

Throughout this process, students' increasing ability to empathize and take perspective is linked more generally to cognitive, social and moral development. As they expand their capacity to hold in mind and use more than one concept at a time, they are more able to consider their own viewpoint and someone else's. As they grow toward adolescence, students' concern for others expands to include the plight of people not known to them personally. Thus, we speak of students' thinking as moving from one-dimensional (one point of view) to multi-dimensional (multiple points of view).

As parents and teachers we don't always wait for students to make discoveries on their own. By creating age-appropriate learning experiences and tasks, teachers can challenge and stretch students' thinking so that they are increasingly able to consider multiple viewpoints. Recognizing that students develop at different rates, teachers can design activities that help each student practice perspective-taking, building from simpler understandings to the more complex, multi-dimensional thinking. Recent research in England and the U.S. shows that, when helped to find a "way in" to history, students are capable of understanding history, including historical perspectives, much younger than previously thought.[7] To provide that "way in," social studies curricula should give students the chance to inquire and solve problems faced by real people.

CULTURE AND PERSPECTIVE-TAKING

We think of culture as a shared pattern of experiences rooted in everyday life. Culture includes people's daily life practices and their beliefs about those practices (i.e. what people do, and how they explain what they do). People are constantly creating culture. Culture is not static, but dynamic.

Many social factors affect a person's daily life and viewpoint: primary among these are race, ethnicity, economic class, and gender. Shared experiences may derive from one's membership in an ethnic or racial group, for example, oral or written traditions, or experiences of discrimination or privilege. Sometimes these different experiences are codified in laws and institutions. For example, South Africans under apartheid were empowered or disempowered based on the color of their skin.

There are also shared experiences that cut across ethnicity or race, that is, that are not based on ethnicity or race alone, but relate to one's economic and social position. These are part of "culture" as well. Poor people have different choices than affluent people.

In the book *Got Me a Story To Tell*, ten-year-old Deltrea recounts how her mother, growing up poor and black in Mississippi, USA, could not go to the same schools as white children, and from the age of seven worked picking cotton for $3.00 a day. She describes listening to her family's stories, and reading about black people who fought for the right to vote, work and grow their own food. Deltrea talks about friendship and "standing up for one another" in her neighborhood and about family members working hard and helping each other. For Deltrea, personal history, African-American history and economic context come together to shape her perspective on the economic and social roles government should play:

8

I want to be President when I grow up...
I'd sit at my desk and they'd say, "President,
could the money be low?"

And I'd say, "Yes, let it be low." That
means you don't have to pay high prices. I would
put cars at $99. That's low 'cause they cost about
a thousand. Everything would be low to four cents.
I would make the train and bus rides low, too.
And I would put the checks up higher and give
people more money to spend. I would take from
the rich and give to the poor. Whoever will
help me, I'll help them. I would make the
world clean, and tell people to stop fighting.

And I'll keep on working till my work is good.[8]

Many people who have struggled to make ends meet might identify with Deltrea's perspective and vote for a candidate who espoused it, regardless of ethnicity. Since *both economic status and ethnicity* shape cultural experience, the activities in this book address both.

In our own classrooms, we recognize that each student comes with a different family, community and school experience, cultural and ethnic heritage and approach to learning. We know that culture affects how students learn, how they interact with others and what they value, as the graphic below illustrates. As teachers we strive to design classroom activities that take these biographies into account. The study of perspectives begins with the self and moves students from their own experience to the experience of others.

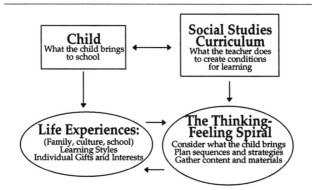

The Interaction Between the Child and the Curriculum

9

Reducing Prejudice Through the Social Studies

As teachers we are faced daily with situations in which students are teased or excluded. Often, the immediate incident has deeper roots: a growing discomfort with differences among peers.

Research shows that young children are aware of racial differences within adult society. As they develop their own identity, children notice differences and begin to make evaluative judgments that are precursors to prejudice. There is evidence that by age two, they use gender labels and color names, associating these names with skin color; by four or five, their play may be gender-differentiated and they may exclude children or select playmates, giving racial reasons. Thus, even at a young age, they may already have begun to internalize adult stereotypes.[9] *why?*

Further, we know that negative attitudes about gender, race and physical disability hurt students as they develop and prevent them from reaching their full potential. Gender stereotyping impacts the emotional and intellectual development of both boys and girls, fostering dependency and inhibiting intellectual risk-taking in girls, and foreclosing experiences in boys. Racism affects the resiliency of minority students and the ability of students in the dominant group to reason and make judgments without distortion. All this hampers students' ability to respond emotionally and intellectually to the world around them.

Students in elementary grades are figuring out who they are and how they feel about themselves and others. Noticing differences is a natural part of development. As Louise Derman-Sparks argues, "It is not the differences in themselves that cause the problem, but how people respond to the differences."[10] Although in the elementary grades students are beginning to associate difference with negatives (reflecting the prejudices of the adults around them), teachers can help students to develop positive attitudes about difference with well-planned curricula. Active intervention can challenge the impact of bias on students' development.

Feeling and thinking must work in concert to reduce prejudice. How we think (cognition), how we feel (affect) and how we act are all dimensions of prejudice. Transmitting "the facts" to passive learners won't by itself create change. Students need to actively make their own meaning within the curriculum. As Nina Gabelko states, "facts do not speak for themselves; rather they are interpreted through the experience and biases of those hearing them."

Curriculum studies suggest two key approaches to prejudice reduction: teaching critical thinking and engaging students in vicarious experiences.[11]

Developing critical thinking skills helps students become open-minded and avoid and distrust the generalizations that lead to stereotypes. Students who learn to observe, question, collect information, reason, and evaluate evidence are less likely to accept stereotypes or assign scapegoats and are more open to changing their own thinking. The activities in this book provide opportunities for students to ask their own questions and investigate them deeply.

Vicarious experience and emotional identification are powerful teachers. They are particularly important for students who do not have much direct contact with members of other racial, ethnic and social groups. Studies found that role-playing or other experiential activities substantially reduce prejudice in youngsters. We know that materials such as films, videos, books and photographs that draw students emotionally into the lives of particular people or characters tend to develop positive attitudes. Students respond when they can identify with the dreams, fears, problems, and feelings of real and fictional characters, if they are realistically and positively portrayed.

Working together to solve common problems and achieve common goals has also been shown to foster positive inter-group attitudes, help students develop more interracial friendships, and even to improve academically. Cooperative learning is a promising approach if tasks are truly cooperative, so that status is equalized within the small groups and students are responsible for teaching, rather than competing with each other.[12] The classroom activities presented in the following chapters apply these prejudice reduction principles to history and social studies.

BRINGING IT ALL TOGETHER

To summarize, empathy and perspective-taking are at the heart of the multicultural curriculum. Thinking and feeling work together to engage students, to motivate them to inquire about another's experience, and to reduce prejudice. Finally, because students learn about the social world through concrete and personal interactions with others, teachers can foster perspective-taking in history with activities that explore social dilemmas in developmentally appropriate ways.

Learning to understand one another is not simple. We all bring our own biographies to learning, including our individual and cultural differences. The further removed another's experience is from our own, the more complex is the task and the more scaffolding we must build to bridge the gap between us. Isolated activities, no matter how powerful, will not meet the challenge. Rather, students need carefully constructed *learning sequences* so that they can build upon earlier understandings by stretching, elaborating and rethinking their assumptions.

The **Thinking-Feeling Spiral**, the curriculum model we use throughout this book, was developed to meet this challenge. Students learn to feel for other people in history (empathize), think about how the world might look through their eyes, and try to explain it (take perspective).

***

Chapter Two presents the **Thinking-Feeling Spiral** in detail. Chapter Three describes six key strategies for developing empathy and perspective-taking which you can use to create learning spirals in your own curriculum context. Part Two (Chapters Four to Seven) demonstrates how to apply the strategies to four major social studies themes: personal history, work, migration and conflict and change. Activities within each theme provide opportunities for students to uncover and come to understand multiple perspectives. You can use the activities as presented, or create your own based on the prototypes we offer.

CHAPTER TWO

THE THINKING-FEELING

SPIRAL

Radio Message to My Best Friend Benja,
   Wherever you are, I miss you. Going to school here is not the same without you. My family has moved so many times, but the hardest was when we had to move away from you and the fields we played in together. We left town in an old truck so that my parents could get work picking melons and fruits. My father played the harmonica all night while we drove and he's teaching me how to play. Someday, when I can see you again, I'll teach you.
   And maybe someday you and I can work in the fields together, take our fruit in a truck to the store, and drive the truck all over the country. Or maybe we could learn how to make houses. My parents tell me we could do that if we study hard.
   Farewell, Benja! I hope you hear me. If you do, send a message to this same radio station, so I know where you are.

Michael

How does Michael, a nine-year-old from an urban center, come to peer through the eyes of a migrant farmworker's son in writing this radio message? In Michael's words, we can hear that he has found a "kernel of like experience"—moving away and missing a friend—that connects him to someone in very different circumstances. He is thinking about what the information he has read about migrant workers might mean in someone else's real life. He imagines how he might feel in a similar situation.

Michael's understanding grew not from one activity, but from a spiral of learning experiences which built upon one another, weaving together opportunities to use information, imagination and feeling. Thinking and feeling were working together here because the curriculum brought them together.

13

The Thinking-Feeling Spiral described in this chapter is a model you can use in your social studies class to help your students develop empathy and perspective-taking skills. The spiral is designed to guide lesson planning. It identifies clusters of activities that help students build their own understandings as they move back and forth between experiencing and reflecting and between thinking about self and thinking about others.

The spiral looks like this:

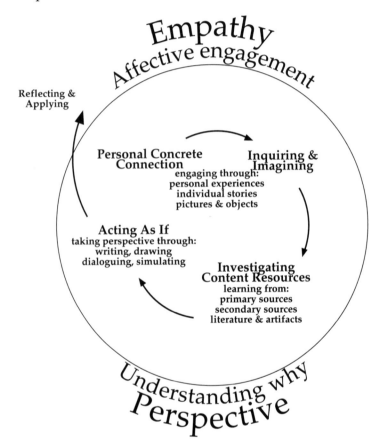

As you can see, the spiral consists of four major kinds of learning experiences: **making personal and concrete connections** to the topic; **inquiring and imagining** about someone else's life; **investigating content resources** to learn more about a group's experience; and **"acting as if"** one is actually in another's circumstances, making choices or solving problems. Each activity in the spiral revolves around key questions and issues for the student.

Why a spiral?

"The spiral is a symbol of growth and learning. It is a process of coming to the same point again and again but at a different level so that everything is seen in a new light."[13]

Jean Piaget and Jerome Bruner, two psychologists who have contributed to our understanding of children's learning, used the metaphor of the cycle or spiral to describe the learning process. They talked about the circular or recursive and ongoing nature of development and learning. Our Thinking-Feeling Spiral builds on their conceptions of children's learning. Our work builds also on Bernice McCarthy's model of curriculum development, which takes into account differences in learning styles.[14]

The expansive vision and writings of John Dewey are the foundation and inspiration for much of the work being done in education today in the areas of prejudice reduction, constructivism and curriculum integration. Our work, too, builds on his thinking about children's learning and the goals of education in an inclusive and democratic society.[15]

MOVING THROUGH THE SPIRAL

• *Making Concrete & Personal Connections*

Students begin the spiral by making a personal connection to the topic, drawing on their own prior knowledge and experience. In the initial activity, the teacher uses concrete objects, an experiential exercise or a personal story and asks **self-related questions**. The teacher's tasks in this part of the spiral are to:

1. identify the human dilemma within the topic to be studied
2. choose a prompt (story, experience, or image) that evokes feelings
3. find the connection to the students' own lives
4. formulate a few beginning self-related questions designed to help students connect something in their own experience to the human problem embedded in the topic:

> – **What do I know or feel about this?**
> – **What does this mean to me?**
> – **Where have I encountered something like this in my life?**

For example, in a study of industrialization, the teacher supposes that her students will be intrigued by exploring the lives of people their own ages who worked in early factories. To begin the spiral, she engages her students in an experiential activity that contextualizes what they are about to study by thinking about work in their own lives. They might interview classmates to find out what chores and after-school jobs they do, how much time they spend working and why they work.

• *Inquiring and Imagining: Shifting from Self to Other*

As students continue through the learning spiral, the teacher serves as a catalyst, moving students from what they know from their own experience to what they imagine is true for someone else in another time or place. The students begin to *inquire about the nature of another's experience,* exploring key **other-related** questions. In the industrialization unit (see the child labor spiral on **p. 18**), the teacher presents the class with a drawing of a child at a loom or a photograph of a child working in a sweatshop in the nineteenth century. Students are asked to imagine who this child is and what her life is like. The concrete prompt (the drawing or photograph) is a catalyst for comparisons between the life of the adolescent in the image and the students in their own class. Juxtaposed with their own experience of work and chores, what these students are discovering about the nineteenth century adolescent may produce some surprises. Previous knowledge and assumptions are challenged, provoking questions and motivating further research.

The teacher's role in this part of the spiral is to:

1. structure a task or introduce a prompt that helps students imagine the life of someone else
2. ask them to grapple with these key **other-related** questions as they work with a concrete object, experience, or story:

   – **Who is this other person?**
   – **What do I imagine her life is like?**
   – **How are we alike? How are we different?**

3. allow students to discuss their imaginings and develop their own questions. For example,

   – Could these children possibly have time for school, homework, and play after having worked for twelve hours?

- Why did children have to work like that?
- Why is your life so different from mine?
- Is this fair?

• *Investigating Content Resources:*
From One Individual Story to the Stories of Many

Motivated by empathy and their own perplexing questions, students begin to gather data, make comparisons, analyze and discuss information. With good resources, the teacher provides opportunities for students to move from thinking about one individual's particular story to considering the collective experience of a group in history through **group-related questions**. What does the experience of *one person* in a photograph or story have to do with history? Why is this important to study? Is it representative of a *collective experience*?

The teacher's role in this part of the spiral is to:

1. introduce source material (such as letters, diaries, eyewitness accounts, songs, literature, or secondary sources)
2. formulate key **group-related** questions for students to grapple with as they research:

- **Is/was life really like this for other people in this group?**
- **How are other people's stories similar to or different from the one I've read about or observed in the photo?**
- **What do I think about this? Is it fair?**

To learn about many examples of people in a similar position to the individuals they've already encountered, students may read autobiographical or biographical sketches, eyewitness accounts, letters or diaries, or view a series of photographs, historical engravings or artifacts. For example, the class studying industrialization now reads eyewitness accounts and letters describing life for children working in various jobs in the nineteenth century, as you can see in the child labor spiral. We emphasize that understanding is based in *content.* Without authentic source material, students hypothesize in a vacuum and run the risk of repeating stereotypes and inaccurate information.

• *"Acting As If...": Empathy and Perspective-Taking in Action*

Students are particularly eager to gather information they are going to use. In this part of the spiral, students *become* a member of a group in history and are asked to *do* something to solve a problem for their group. Using all the information they have been gathering, they write, draw, dialogue or simulate what it would be like to make decisions on behalf of someone else. Students at this part of the spiral go *beyond* empathy to take another's perspective. They must *explain* events, action, and decisions in the first person voice of their assumed identity, and respond to **"acting as if…"** questions.

The teacher's role in this part of the spiral is to:

1. set up specific tasks or experiences which call upon students to solve problems and make decisions through the eyes of another group
2. formulate key "acting as if…" questions

> **– How would I have felt in your position?**
> **– How would I have seen or explained this?**
> **– What would I do/decide?**

The students studying industrialization are asked to "act as if…" they worked in a mill or sweatshop in the nineteenth century. The teacher tells them there is a Labor Commission investigating the conditions of work for children and making recommendations for new labor laws. If workers talk to the investigators they could be fired. Should they risk their jobs and talk? What laws are needed to protect child workers?

Child-Labor Spiral

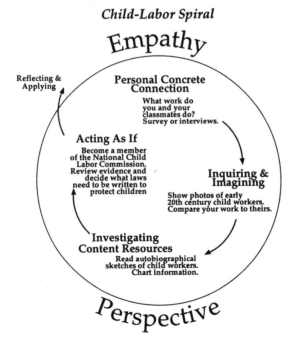

Empathy

Reflecting & Applying

Personal Concrete Connection
What work do you and your classmates do? Survey or interviews.

Acting As If
Become a member of the National Child Labor Commission. Review evidence and decide what laws need to be written to protect children

Inquiring & Imagining
Show photos of early 20th century child workers. Compare your work to theirs.

Investigating Content Resources
Read autobiographical sketches of child workers. Chart information.

Perspective

A Pattern of Questions: The Key to the Spiral

Key to the spiral is a **developmental pattern of questions: self-related questions, other-related questions, group-related questions and "acting as if..." questions.** This pattern fosters empathy in the social studies by helping students find common ground between themselves and others. The questions are bridges that enable students to reach into the past, to people and places far from their immediate realm of experience. Following the model of the Thinking-Feeling Spiral, the questioning pattern begins with students' own lives and gradually moves them from thinking about their experience to thinking about the experience of another, and then from one individual's story to the history of many. In this process, the abstract nature of history and social studies seems more real and concrete. As you engage your students in finding out "why and how" through the questioning pattern, you model the kinds of questions real historians ask. Although the pattern of questioning can be adapted to almost any social studies topic, specific questions are tailored to each lesson.

Notice that all the questions within the four major learning experiences of the spiral are open-ended—they cannot be answered by a "yes" or "no." They invite students to respond in many different ways, drawing on their own understandings. When you pose a question that raises a discrepancy between what the students already think and what they are now discovering, students may be puzzled. This puzzlement, or dissonance, provokes interest and sets in motion the need to find out more. Soon students begin asking their own "real" questions. The pattern of questions is used with many strategies throughout the book.

The rest of this book demonstrates the "how to" of the Thinking-Feeling spiral. The next chapter describes specific strategies to use within the spiral. Part Two (Chapters Four through Seven) takes you through activities that demonstrate how the spiral works with key history and social studies topics. We hope that you will find our prototype activities useful in designing your own.

· · · · · · · · · · · · · ·

CHAPTER THREE

WHEN CHILDREN CARE:

STRATEGIES FOR

PERSPECTIVE-TAKING

To understand the perspective of people living in a time or situation removed from their own personal experience, students must become personally engaged with the subject matter— they must care. When students care, they develop a need to know, which is a motivation for gathering and interpreting data and testing out their views in interaction with their peers.

The six major strategies described in this chapter create classroom opportunities for students to actively construct their understandings of another's point of view. These strategies can be used at various times in the learning sequence. Part Two presents activity exemplars which demonstrate how to use the six strategies with four key social studies themes.

Perspectives Through Primary Sources

What do we mean by primary sources? A primary source is created by an eyewitness to or a participant in an event in history. It can be a written document such as a letter or journal, a photograph or an object from times past. Jan West, editor of Cobblestone's *Teaching with Primary Sources Series*, writes: "When students research in original sources, they find the pulse and breath of people long dead and they begin to be curious about these people, empathize with them and care about their fates."[16] You can create conversations between students in your classroom and peoples of other times and circumstances by working with primary sources.

There are three main types of primary sources:

1. artifacts
2. photographs
3. documents (letters, diaries, etc.)

ARTIFACTS: "TALKING OBJECTS"

What do we mean by artifacts? Artifacts are authentically from the time, place or culture you are studying. They include the collectibles, mementos and memorabilia preserved from times past, such as old-fashioned appliances, toys or articles of clothing. Authentic materials are sometimes difficult to attain, expensive or too fragile to endure students' handling. Many other kinds of objects, sometimes known as "realia," are equally powerful in promoting perspective-taking in the classroom. These include folk arts and crafts, facsimiles (replicas, posters or reproductions such as one might find in a souvenir shop) and some of the objects we use in daily life.

Artifacts speak to us when we ask questions. In this book we demonstrate ways you can create "conversations" between students and artifacts to help students visualize lives and discover stories of the past. Like historians and anthropologists, your students can ask the artifacts to tell stories about the people who used them. They construct interpretations, explanations and hypotheses based on concrete evidence with questions such as:

- **What is this object? How would I use it?**
- **Do I have something like it at my house?**
- **How would my daily life be different if I worked or played with this?**
- **What does this tell me about the people who used this/made this/worked with this?**
- **How are their lives similar to or different from mine?**
- **What if only some people were allowed to wear it or use it?**

"Talking Objects" is a strategy that utilizes play, the language of childhood. In real life, children learn about their world through playing with all kinds of everyday objects: dolls, building blocks, cars, dress-up clothes. In the classroom, historical objects can be a natural link between the concrete world of students and the more abstract realms of history and culture. Artifacts and objects talk to the students about the daily lives of people of other times, places, cultural or economic backgrounds. Using their senses, students imaginatively play with ideas about what it might have been like to use this hollowed-out wooden bucket, work in these overalls, carry this bundle. Students talk with one another about their playful reconstructions of life. History becomes a story of "regular people."

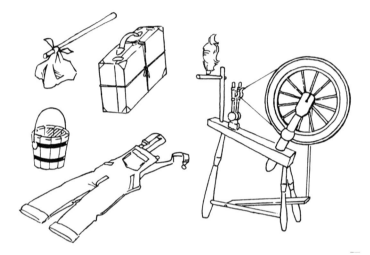

What strikes each student about an object is different. For example, a teacher might bring a farm tool to class. One student may have used a tool like it, another may have seen one in a museum, still another may be intrigued by how it works, though he or she might never have seen anything like it before. The farm tool does more than engage the students' imaginations. It engages each student's personal storehouse of relevant knowledge, helping her find a personal "point of entry" into the learning spiral, so necessary for empathy and perspective-taking.

"Talking Objects" activities in this book include "The Personal History Suitcase" and "Family Heritage Stories." These activities are prototypes you can adapt to design activities in your own curriculum.

PHOTOGRAPHS: "TALKING PICTURES"

When the Red River flooded in 1997, threatening to destroy thousands of houses in Canada and the United States, people frantically gathered up their most valuable possessions. At the top of most people's list were family photographs. Why do we attach such meaning to photographs in our lives?

Photographs preserve a part of our own history as nothing else can. They freeze a moment in time, give us an opportunity "to be there" once again. In social studies, photographs have an important role to play. They provide a rich source of historical information, particularly about the lives of peoples who did not write history books and whose history is often "hidden." Photographs also offer a direct affective experience that spawns empathy. They help students reach out to distant times and circumstances, seeing the human beings who inhabit worlds unlike their own as people like themselves, rather than as abstractions. The almost palpable impact, for example, of a photograph showing would-be gold miners lined up for miles waiting to ascend a steep ridge—some of them giving in to exhaustion and frostbite and sliding back down the mountain—puts a human face on our textbook knowledge of the Alaska-Klondike Gold Rush.

As with artifacts, photographs talk to us when we ask questions. They also provoke questions. Students can interact with photographs, observing, reacting, imagining, and dialoguing with the people in the pictures. They look carefully at the content of the photographic image, at the objects, surroundings, clothing, people's expressions, gestures and actions. Students are asked to imagine what the people in the photograph are doing, thinking, feeling, and then to cite evidence as to how they know this. They put words to the photograph, creating dialogue between people or interviewing someone in the picture.

An activity in this book that uses the "Talking Pictures" strategy is "Children At Work."

DOCUMENTS: LETTERS, DIARIES AND JOURNALS

Because the stories and voices of ordinary people are often absent from history texts, many students believe that what their ancestors did wasn't important enough to appear in the history books. Students may feel similarly that they have little impact on history.

Where can our students find accounts of ordinary people? "Fortunately," writes Jacqueline Katz in her book, *Making Our Way: America at the Turn of the Century in the Words of the Poor and Powerless*, "despite formidable handicaps, ordinary people did leave a written heritage.... People wrote letters to newspapers, unions and one another. Some kept diaries and a few wrote books."[17] These sources of information bring an ordinary person from another time or place to life, with the rich details that help students visualize another reality.

When someone tells about an experience in his or her own words, he or she invites an intimacy. Students reading primary documents come to know the writer, not as a distanced character, but as a friend sharing personal thoughts and feelings. They are more able to see through the eyes of the other in the context of the writer's life and circumstances. Journals, diaries, letters and interviews can be particularly powerful in helping students empathize and take the perspective of others. In the example below, Sadie Fromme's diary entry describes her daily struggles with the dangers of the machines in the sweatshop:

> *So I went to work in Allen Street (Manhattan) in what they call a sweatshop, making skirts by machine. I was new at the work and the foreman scolded me a great deal.*

> *The machines go like mad all day, because the faster you work the more money you get. Sometimes in my haste I get my finger caught and the needle goes right through it. It goes so quick tho, that it does not hurt much. I bind the finger up with a piece of cotton and go on working. We all have accidents like that. Where the needle goes through the nail it makes a sore finger, or where it splinters a bone it does much harm. Sometimes a finger has to come off. Generally, tho, one can be cured by a salve.[18]*

Using authentic source material, students work like historians, asking questions and making inferences. Why did Sadie go on working when she hurt her finger? Why did she have to work faster and not more carefully? Why did she get scolded about her work even though she was new at the job? What did she get to do after work? Through primary sources, they can also compare lives of individuals from diverse groups and various times, using the questioning pattern. Did all girls work like Sadie at the turn of the century? How did people live then? What has changed and why? Students learn that people did think differently, and that there were reasons why they did so. They become active seekers of information rather than passive consumers of facts.

Activities that use the letter/diary/journal strategy are: "Snapshots of My Life in a New Country," "Radio Message Center," and "The Trail of Tears."

Perspectives Through Children's Literature

By omissions or by one-sided presentations of issues, textbooks can leave students with the idea that there is only one version of the past, rather than bringing them into the historical discussion. Good children's fiction can present in a dramatic and personal form the lives and views of ordinary people often invisible in texts. These are our students' historical counterparts. Through historical fiction, our students may also "live history" through other children of different circumstances, leading them to "recreate" historical events through the characters' eyes. If students are asked to interact with the story and characters, fiction can bridge the students' world and the world of other groups and other times, uncovering multiple viewpoints.

What perspectives *are* there to uncover in history? And *what is it* that makes people view things differently and act differently? Does it matter if you are a boy or girl, man or woman, rich or poor, Black, white or aboriginal, land-owner or wage-laborer? For example, in the period of the American Revolution, when women had few legal and economic rights, did women define "freedom" the same way as men? What if you were a Black woman in that period? Students can begin to wrestle with these types of questions in concrete ways through story.

The challenge, of course, is to choose literature carefully. We look for good literature with an authentic voice (authors of the same ethnicity, gender or economic background as their protagonists). We want books with characters who exemplify "hidden" perspectives (voices of women, the poor, minorities). We also seek out stories which develop conflicting viewpoints on the same events.

Three techniques are particularly helpful in working with literature:

- focusing on critical decision-making moments
- using parallel stories on the same theme
- combining literature with primary and secondary sources

FOCUSING ON CRITICAL DECISION-MAKING MOMENTS

Historical fiction can dramatically portray the impact of major conflicts, social changes or events on people's lives. *Focusing on critical decision-making moments in the story* allows students to glimpse how race, gender, wealth or other differences shape people's feelings and decisions. Students are jettisoned into the drama of history as they help characters resolve their dilemmas, coming to understand how they themselves might feel, view events and act in similar circumstances. The character's personal dilemma raises broader social issues for children now and then. For example, in the activity "No Loyal Citizen," students wrestle with how discriminatory social policies affect people, and what "rights" and "responsibilities" mean in a democracy.

Activities that focus on critical decision-making moments are: "No Loyal Citizen" and "The Snow Tiger."

USING PARALLEL STORIES ON THE SAME THEME

While a good piece of fiction can portray the human drama of history, it often tells the story in the context of one person's life. Building social studies concepts, on the other hand, requires that we go beyond one individual's story. What do our stories have in common that makes up a collective history? Can literature help students answer this question? Reading a series of picture books about different migration experiences, war experiences, or work experiences can help students see that many individuals share parts of a common story. Further, we can see a piece of ourselves in these stories. They are in some way connected to our own family experiences, perhaps several generations back. In this book we use several pieces of fiction related to the same theme so that students can explore similarities and differences in a collective history.

Activities that use stories on the same theme are: "A Stitch in Time" and "Story Cloths."

COMBINING PRIMARY AND SECONDARY SOURCES WITH CHILDREN'S FICTION

In the book *Radio Man* by Arthur Dorros, Diego's family moves many times in a month in order to follow the harvest and continue to get work picking crops in the fields. Students might ask questions such as: Do migrant workers really have to move that often? How is Diego's experience similar to that of people around the world who harvest crops for others? Although students can identify with the struggles and courage of characters in fiction, it still *is* fiction, and may be more or less accurate in its portrayal. In addition, it is focused on the experience of individual characters, who may or may not be representative of a group of people.

26

To move from the experience of one individual to understanding the experience of a group of people, students need additional data. They need to inquire about similarities and differences among members of the same group, compare sources and draw conclusions. We advocate using primary sources (artifacts, letters, interviews, diaries, autobiographies) and secondary materials (including texts) along with the fiction. This connects fiction to the real world. It adds detail and context, engages the visual and sensory imagination, and allows students to compare many examples and question accuracy.

Activities that combine fiction with primary and secondary sources are: "The Snow Tiger" and "Radio Message Center."

PERSPECTIVES THROUGH WRITING

The Power of Personal Writing

We write in order to express feelings or talk to people we love about our daily lives, important events, or things that concern us. Writing in the social studies can make use of this natural avenue of expression to foster empathy and perspective-taking.

The following writing forms are used in activities throughout the book. You will notice that our writing activities begin with a prompt and ask students to solve a problem. A prompt can be a piece of fiction, a work of art, a question, a statement, a quotation, or an experiential activity. The prompt helps students identify opposing viewpoints and feelings. Figuring out what it would have been like "had I been there..." often involves students in descriptive writing as well, answering questions like "what would I see? hear? feel?"

First person writing is powerful strategy. Assuming the voice of another person, students construct a bridge across time and circumstance, imagining themselves with the hopes, dreams, difficulties and dilemmas of other peoples. Based on real historical information provided by the teacher, students "recreate" a person of different circumstances within themselves, a person "like myself" and "not like myself" at the same time. They "humanize" and evaluate historical information in light of real lives.

Quick Response Writing

These are "free-writes"—brief, reactive pieces that help students connect by thinking about something in their own experience that is related to the social studies concept to be studied. For example, students may be asked to recall a time when they felt they were treated unfairly, or felt different. They then jot down feelings or thoughts about those moments. Quick response writing is illustrated in the activity "The Personal History Suitcase."

Letters

Students can explore perspectives in history through letter-writing. Letters might be written between or to:

- characters in historical fiction
- real or fictional people in history and someone they miss
- a contemporary person and an historical person
- a community organization or government agency

We illustrate letter and message writing activities in "Radio Message Center."

Perspectives Poetry

We use two forms of poetry in developing perspectives: *monologue poems* and *dialogue poems*. In a monologue poem, different participants in the same event write monologues. Each monologue has a choral line which expresses a key message and is repeated periodically throughout the poem. In a dialogue poem, two characters speak about a common experience from two opposing viewpoints. The poem contains several common lines, read by both the characters together. "Newcomers in Our Town" uses powerful poetic counterpoint to contrast the viewpoints, hopes and fears of newly-arrived immigrant families and old town residents in one community's reaction to increased immigration.

Personal History Narratives

Here students take the voice of a relative and write their own or another family's migration story (one of their classmate's perhaps). In "Family Heritage Stories," each student writes in the voice of a partner's family member, producing a class book of family histories.

Journals and Diaries

In journal and diary writing, students answer the questions "How might these historical events affect the person writing this journal? How might the person affect the events?" Although journal and diary writing are often given as one-time assignments, in real life thoughts and feelings change. "The Snow Tiger" illustrates how students can synthesize different sources of information (fiction, primary source material, textbooks) to write in-depth personal journals over time.

Sentence Stems

Using sentence stems, students assume the voice of a person or group in history, and complete a thought in response to teacher prompts. Sentence stems might include:

> I think…/I feel…/I need…/I wonder…
> Things would be better/different if…
> We don't understand…

In "The Trail of Tears," after reading first-hand accounts of the Cherokee removal from their homeland, students voice the views of soldiers, Cherokees, government officials and settlers by completing sentence stems.

Writing Dialogues

Different views of the *same* historical event can be explored through imaginative dialogues. These may be dialogues between characters in a novel or picture book, or between real historical personages students read about in non-fiction sources.

Students create dialogues in "No Loyal Citizen."

"What if…?" Writing

Could history have taken a different course? In "what if …" assignments, students answer the question: What would have happened had we done something different at a particularly important historical moment? They explore alternative scenarios and write a new chapter in history. "What if…?" writing assignments occur in "The Buddha Statue" and in "The Trail of Tears."

Group Experience Writing

Here the whole class together writes a "history" of what happened during an experiential activity in class, perhaps a role play or simulation. Like real historians, they reconstruct something that actually happened, synthesizing what they've learned. Since everyone in the class has experienced the same event and the class maps out the essay collectively, group experience writing helps a range of writers, including second language learners.

In "People in the Revolution," for example, the class mind-maps and writes from the perspectives of different groups of men and women represented in their classroom simulation.

How does art help our students to understand human dilemmas and express their feelings about the world? The arts and other visual tools are invaluable in developing empathy and perspective-taking. Learning styles and multiple intelligence experts embrace the idea of providing alternative ways for students to learn new things and to express what they know. When many forms of representation are available for students, they can tap into the richness of human experience compassionately and thoughtfully.

The Fine Arts

"My Precious Water, I Kiss You" by Parkpoom Poompana, Age 15. Grand Prize—1996 River of Words Environmental Poetry and Art Contest © 1996 International Rivers Network

Consider how the painting shown above affects you. You can *feel* the artist's deep appreciation for our natural resources because the painting invites you to share the intimacy and tenderness of the kiss. Viewing the painting also evokes questions about how the artist came to create this compassionate piece. Why is water so important to him?

The arts embrace a different way of coming to know. As Nancy Flowers states in *Human Rights Education and the Arts:*

> *...the arts can serve to tap the rich resources of the heart and stimulate moral imagination, an essential for citizenship. What is it like to be a refugee? What is the nature of justice? How can I convey to others my understanding of human dignity? How can I live out human rights values in my own life? Music, poetry, drama and the graphic arts can provide students with the means to formulate their own questions and explore their answers.* [19]

The arts hold a special place in the development of cross-cultural understandings. Working with art forms from many cultures and historical periods, students discover how a people's art connects to their daily life, environment, social organization or traditions. We use the arts in several ways to develop empathy and perspective-taking:

- viewing and responding to art
- creating art (drawing and painting)
- voicing views through drama

Viewing Art

When looking at art, students often respond emotionally. Asked to pay attention to details in the art work, they begin to grasp larger social studies concepts—concepts like migration, urbanization, social inequality and the relationship between people and the environment—in concrete and personal ways. For example, George Littlechild's painting "A Red Horse in a Sea of White Horses" in the book *This Land is My Land* visually represents a Plains Cree North American Indian view of history. In it we see the pain and alienation of Native peoples in the wake of European encroachment. This painting is about Littlechild's experience in an all-white school.

> *In this picture, an Indian warrior sits atop a red horse. Not at home in his own territory, this red horse lives among the white horses who find him different and don't understand him. The red horse is taught that he is always wrong and whites are always right. That is why the check marks appear on the white horses. The red horse represents me.* [20]

Several activities in this book illustrate ways to help students understand another's experience by observing art closely and noticing particulars.

Creating Art

In creating art, students express what they know in nonverbal ways. In her book *Going Beyond Words*, Kathy Mason adapts Rudolph Arnheim's work in visual thinking.[21] She describes three visual thinking modes: see, imagine, and draw. These three processes encourage a special kind of paying attention which captures feelings as well as ideas. We have used them in the activities "Owls and Jobs," and "Wishes and Dreams."

The Dramatic Arts

Voicing views through dramatic arts is another key perspective-taking strategy. When students role play, they speak as if they were someone from history. They take on the feelings and thoughts of someone else; their peers may take on different roles from that time or place. Together they recreate the context for decision-making that helps them understand why people acted as they did.

The activities "People in the Revolution" and "Newcomers in Our Town" both require students to role-play different perspectives.

VISUAL TOOLS

The activities in this book use mind maps and other graphic organizers in various parts of the Thinking-Feeling Spiral to help develop empathy and perspective-taking. Mind maps, charts, matrices and diagrams aid students in gathering and organizing information. Visual representations allow students to hold on to ideas and feelings as they actively talk, compare and question. As Julie Cowell says, visual tools help students to brainstorm, categorize, classify, see relationships, organize, personalize, enrich and to combine any of the preceding processes.[22] We highlight two major purposes for the use of visual tools in developing empathy and perspective-taking. The first relates to *capturing initial feelings*. The second purpose relates to *recording and comparing information*.

Mind Maps

Consider how the following example of a mind map activity provided a way for students to literally see what they and others knew, thought and felt about the elderly. Students were asked to write the word "grandmothers" in a circle in the center of a piece of paper, to add five or six circles around the center word, and in each circle quickly write a word that came to mind. As we can see from the class's diagram below, this initial activity revealed a stereotypical view of grandmothers.

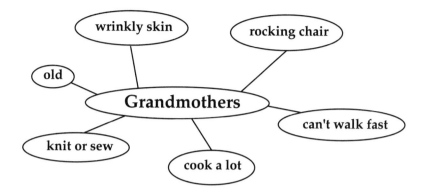

The next day students were asked to write the words "My Grandmother" in the center of a new sheet of paper, to think about the following questions in relation to their *own* grandmothers, and to write some words on this second mind map.

- *What does your grandmother look like? What does she like to do for fun?*
- *Where do you go with your grandmother? Does she have a job?*
- *Does your grandmother plant things? Who are your grandmother's friends?*
- *Where does your grandmother live? What does your grandmother laugh at, get mad at, get sad about?*

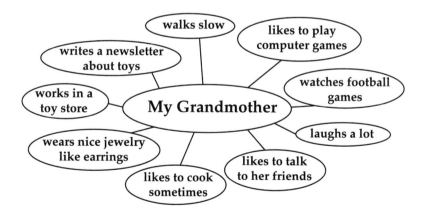

The students then looked for differences and similarities between the two mind maps. They looked at the stereotypical words from the first mind map, applied them to their grandmothers, and saw where the stereotypes fit and where they did not. Students wrote essays about their grandmothers and made a class book. The visual tools assisted them in recalling and representing their experience so that they could go on, in further unit activities, to explore some ways that stereotypes are formed, and how stereotypical thinking stands in the way of understanding other perspectives.

In the activity "A Stitch in Time," students use a mind map to capture first thoughts about quilts and what they mean to them.

Charts, Matrices and Venn Diagrams

A second purpose of visual tools is to display information and juxtapose content from a variety of sources. Visual tools for this purpose include charts, matrices and Venn diagrams. The visuals allow the students to hold on to detailed information as they actively grapple with it. They look for patterns, find similarities and differences and synthesize information. Thus the visual becomes an analytical tool.

In the activity "Children at Work," students construct a Child Work Data Chart comparing lives of child workers in various jobs:

	Age	Hours of work	Why they work	Kind of work	Effect on education	Health hazards
Child's name						
Child's name						
Child's name						

Venn diagrams also serve this purpose of comparing and contrasting, as students think about how someone may be *like them* and *not like them*. In the activity "Snapshots of Life in my New Country," students create a Venn diagram to compare problems they have faced to problems that Shirmani, a recent immigrant to this country is facing.

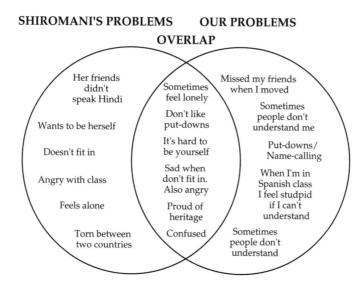

SHIROMANI'S PROBLEMS   **OUR PROBLEMS**

OVERLAP

Her friends didn't speak Hindi

Wants to be herself

Doesn't fit in

Angry with class

Feels alone

Torn between two countries

Sometimes feel lonely

Don't like put-downs

It's hard to be yourself

Sad when don't fit in. Also angry

Proud of heritage

Confused

Missed my friends when I moved

Sometimes people don't understand me

Put-downs/ Name-calling

When I'm in Spanish class I feel studpid if I can't understand

Sometimes people don't understand

Experiencing History

PERSONAL HISTORY INVESTIGATIONS

When my grampa Dave was a little boy, he had to get dressed next to the stove because they had no heat.

My grandpa didn't even have a TV when he grew up. He listened to the radio. "The Shadow" was his favorite program—"Lights out, everybody!"

My aunt slept in the same room as her five sisters. They lived in a small apartment. She got sick and almost died when she was small. When she got well, my grandma gave her a new name, Gladys, which means, "Glad is my heart."

Students are interested in family stories. In searching for their family stories, heirlooms and memorabilia, they come to see themselves as a part of history. Sharing their histories in the classroom builds a bridge from the present to the past and between themselves and the other students.

Personal History Investigations build the skills that are the foundation of historical thinking. Students work with history much as historians do. In the process they are learning to:

- understand chronology
- construct a narrative based on evidence

- build multiple explanations
- hypothesize about the influences of the past on the present

In Part Two, Chapter Four "Through our Memories," students probe the meaning of culture and history in their own lives. They investigate commonalities and differences in the stories of their classmates and their families, and begin to see history as the collective stories and decisions of many individuals just like themselves. As they identify commonalities in peoples' hopes, fears and dreams, they take a step toward empathy. As they recognize differences in circumstances and choices, they try to understand the reasons for other people's actions. This is the beginning of perspective-taking. The "Family Heritage Stories" activity enables students to "experience" history, learning about culture in individually meaningful ways.

HISTORIAN'S SIMULATION WORKSHOP

As students move on in the social studies, they are asked to venture further away from their own direct experiences and those of people they know. Why should an eleven-year-old care about ancient Egyptians? Many creative teachers struggle daily with such questions as they implement history curriculum guidelines. They know that the farther students go from their personal story, the more vehicles the teacher needs to provide to make them care about historical persons and events.

Historian's Simulation Workshop focuses on problem-solving in history. Students are asked to make critical decisions for a group of people in history. In simulation, students are motivated through peer interaction and problem-solving to reconstruct the dynamics of historical events. They become emotionally invested in the plight of historical persons because of their interactions with other students in the class as they role play. As they develop "a need to know," they read sources and gather information about the circumstances, options and fears of their group. Guided by a series of critical-thinking questions, they explore possible alliances with other groups. Then they are asked to make—and justify—decisions. Afterwards, they compare the history they created in the classroom to the history that really occurred. Unanswered questions become the basis for further research and writing.

The Historian's Simulation Workshop is a wonderful way to investigate multiple perspectives on the same event, particularly during times of turbulence and rapid change. In such times, underlying social tensions and goals are dramatically revealed. How is it that participants in the same event can see things so differently? What in their experience filters their view? Admittedly, these are sophisticated concepts. But students can wrestle with them, given concrete materials and interactive methods.

In the activity "People in the Revolution," students assume the roles of different ethnic, gender and economic groups in two revolutions. Using this simulation as a prototype, you can find applications in your own curriculum, and create simulations about many periods of conflict and change, including: the French Revolution, 20th century labor strikes, the Chinese Revolution, the United States Civil War and Women's Suffrage.

***

The activities in Part Two are organized in chapters under the broad social studies themes of Personal and Family History, Work, Migration, and Conflict and Change. Each activity demonstrates how to use one or more of the strategies described in this chapter. We hope you use the strategies to create Thinking-Feeling Spirals suited to the needs of your students and your curriculum.

PART TWO *Social Studies Themes and Activities*

CHAPTER FOUR

THROUGH OUR MEMORIES

Perspective-taking activities

Introduction

W̲e begin building multicultural perspectives through our memories and personal histories. The Thinking-Feeling Spiral begins with the personal, and what is more personal than stories of childhood? Favorite bedtime stories everywhere begin with the words, "When I was a little girl..." and "When I was just about your age . . ." Children are entertained by the hour listening to relatives tell and retell childhood stories and they listen with rapture to stories of their own babyhood. These stories help students form first pictures of times past. Through the memories of their own parents, grandparents, and relatives, students begin to understand how the past was different from today, that their grandparents did not watch TV, for instance, or even necessarily have a radio. They also discover that in many ways, there are commonalities in childhood experiences across time and place.

In this chapter, students enter the world of the past through their own history, their teacher's personal history, and through the eyes of their classmates and their families. In these ways, they make crucial connections to the idea that the past has something to do with their own lives in the present. They also begin to take perspectives across cultures as they listen to these stories and try taking the role of someone who is different from themselves. Students' motivation in history and social studies often depends on their building personal connections. The activities in this chapter help students see commonalities so they are able to build their own bridges across the differences.

This chapter presents three approaches to personal history investigations: through one's own life history, through family stories, and through children's literature. In these activities, students move through the Thinking-Feeling Spiral, making personal connections, asking their own questions, learning about others' experiences, and "acting as if" they were in another's place.

Activity #1
THE PERSONAL HISTORY SUITCASE:
HANDS-ON HISTORY

Topic: Perspective-taking through personal history artifacts

Age: Suitable for all ages

Concepts:
- Developing point of view in history
- Making personal connections with history

Strategies:
- Personal History Investigations
- Artifacts: "Talking Objects"
- Quick Response Writing

Resources:
- Objects from the teacher's childhood
- Books about collections of personal history (see bibliography)

Activity Profile: Using objects from her own childhood, the teacher helps students see the past through her eyes, using personal artifacts to introduce them to the idea of perspectives in history. The suitcase contains items selected by the teacher to represent her childhood: a prized toy, a memento from a relative, a "fad" item such as a Captain Marvel ring or a Beatles decal. One by one, she shows the items to her students, who ask questions to learn about each object, such as: "Why did you like that doll so much?" "Who read that book to you?" "Was there a special reason why your mother gave you that?" "How old were you?" "Where did you live?" Later in the activity, when students describe what stood out to them, they find that each of them has a different perspective and interpretation of what they have seen and heard. They may say, "our teacher is a sentimental person," "she likes to share her old things," or "she liked to sing." Each statement made by each individual student bears the signature of the student who said it. Students see that the story—or history—of their teacher's childhood may depend on who is telling the story and that the story may differ from storyteller to storyteller.

STEPS

Step 1. Introduce students to the suitcase, telling them it contains objects from your childhood that they will be able to look at and hold. Explain that in order for them to find out about each object, they must ask good questions.

Step 2. Brainstorm questions to ask the teacher. Help students recognize the difference between questions that have "yes" or "no" answers and questions that are open-ended. Examples might be: "Why did you save that hat all these years?" versus "did you like that hat?" Help students brainstorm questions beginning with "why," "how" and "what," which tend to produce more information. Have students practice their questioning with a few objects in the room.

Step 3. Show students items from your suitcase. Explain that there is a story connected to each object. By including items that represent a memory or activity from your childhood, such as a favorite food, you will emphasize the importance of the memory over the material possession. Simply name each item: "This is a _____ that my mother gave me." Invite students to ask questions. Answer the questions briefly. You can show all the objects or present them one or two a day each day for a week. Depending on the age and skill level of your students, you may want to develop note-taking and other writing skills by asking students to record their responses in a graphic organizer such as a chart or mind map.

Step 4. At the conclusion of the activity, ask your students to write, draw or say something about what "stood out" for them. They might try writing your biography, beginning with an introductory sentence or statement such as, "Nancy was...." Older students might write your biography in greater depth, filling in the details as they imagine them based on the information from the activity. Comparing the biographies leads to insights on the work of historians and the uses of evidence.

Esther Dane, age 5

Step 5. Students share their ideas. Remind students that they all saw and heard the same information. Discuss possible explanations for the differences in their statements. Ask, "why do you think you had such different ways of telling about me? Why do you think different things stood out to you?" Talk about how each of us comes to new experiences with different backgrounds, interests, likes and dislikes which influence how we view and interpret what happens. Ask them to extend their thoughts about this experience to history in the larger sense, to the explanations given for events and decisions of the past. Explain that when historians write about "what happened," what they write is very often influenced in the same way. This can lead to interesting discussions about what "history" is.

Ideas for follow-up activities

This activity leads to a wide variety of investigations, both personal and historical. Here are just a few ideas:

- **Point of view in other historical sources:** Students can pose these questions when reading an historical document, a diary or newspaper article: "Who wrote this? What is his or her point of view? What is another point of view? How does the author's point of view influence his or her account of what happened?"
- **Student history suitcases:** Students create their own history suitcases (from shoe boxes, for example). Note: This is different from a family heritage activity, which focuses on prior generations.
- **Timelines:** Model how to make a timeline by creating a timeline of your own life using artifacts and stories from your suitcase. Students then make their own "personal history timelines." These can be done as drawings, paintings, collages, cartoon strips, or videos.
- **Museum display:** Students set up a "museum" to display and share their personal histories through artifacts.
- **Searching for patterns:** Create a visual organizer to look for any patterns and generalizations among class members' personal histories, and to generate questions for further study of topics of interest, such as children's games and toys, popular music in another era, etc.

Activity #2
FAMILY HERITAGE STORIES:
MY HISTORY, YOUR HISTORY, OUR HISTORY

Topic:	Family heritage
Age:	8 and up
Concepts:	• Making personal connections with history • Multiple perspectives on a common theme • Finding commonalities and differences between self and others, finding the collective story of the past
Strategies:	• Artifacts: "Talking Objects" • Personal History Investigations • Writing Personal History Narratives • Visual Tools
Resources:	Heritage objects brought by students

Activity Profile: Students learn about the past by looking through the eyes of their own ancestors. They collect information about their family's history, and bring to class an object that represents their heritage. Listening to one another's stories, they discover similarities. They then write in the first person the story of a partner's relative and create a class book of family histories. This activity builds personal connections with the past as students uncover the collective story of many individuals who have shaped history.

Step 1. (Preparation): Tell students that they are going to learn about their family history by choosing and sharing an object from home that represents their heritage. Encourage students to be creative and resourceful in choosing their objects which could range, for example, from an inexpensive heirloom to an old letter. You can tailor this activity to suit the needs and circumstances of your class. For instance, since many families do not or cannot save material objects, you can affirm a variety of ways for students to participate. You might suggest bringing an object that represents a family tradition or favorite story. When you model the activity, be sure to emphasize the acceptability of a simple or symbolic object that stands for something like a family ritual.

Step 2. (Preparation): Brainstorm with your class a list of questions to ask parents and relatives so that students can tell the story that goes with the object. Discuss with the class what information would be interesting and useful to find out. This might include: How does the object tell a story about your family? Why is it important in your family? What was the object used for? What is the journey the object took? What do we know about the people who passed it on to us? When did family members come to this country or region? Why did they leave to come here?

Step 3. Model the activity by sharing one item from your own family history. Briefly tell the story that goes with the object, including the kind of information you want your students to include when they share their own objects. For example, you can structure the information around chronology, immigration, family occupation, family traditions, etc.

Step 4. Students bring their objects to school. Each student has a chance to share with the whole class. This part of the activity can take several days. As the students share, the teacher asks for similarities and differences in the stories, and records them in categories on a chalkboard or on paper.

Step 5. Students now begin the process of preparing to put together a class book of family histories. Pair students with a partner, and tell them that they will write their piece for the book as if they were their partner's ancestor. They will need to remember that ancestor's story. Then have students help one another retell their stories in a structured way. Each student interviews his or her partner, using the questions that were developed earlier. For younger students, "idea boxes" such as the one shown below can be used to help organize the information.

Where and when did the journey begin?	Who brought or used the object? Who started this tradition?
Why did they leave? Why come here?	What work did they do?

Step 6. After the interviews, each student writes a chapter of a class book from the point of view of his or her partner's family member. Each student writes in the first person as if she were her partner's family member telling the heritage story.

Step 7. You can model this first person writing by reading a short story like the one below.

Miriam's Story

I am Miriam, Moses' and Esther's great great grandmother. I learned to be a midwife in the town of Lemberg, Poland. It was women who mostly helped deliver babies back then. Most women learned how to be midwives from other midwives, but sometimes they went to school to learn. This is my diploma from the college of midwifery I went to. I was married to a tailor named Herman. When we came to America only five of my children survived. I wanted them to stay in school and not have to work as children, so I had to work very hard to help support the family. I was very proud when all five of my sons graduated from college. My oldest son, Isidor, was Moses' and Esther's great grandfather.

Step 8. Put all the stories together in a class book for your class library. Have students illustrate the stories, working in their pairs or alone.

Ideas for extension activities

Family History Interview: Students may interview family members to gather other sorts of historical information about what life was like in the past. They may find out about childhood games, toys and pastimes of their parents and extended family members, and what fads existed then. They may construct surveys about anything they want to learn about: clothing, television viewing, radio, popular music, household appliances, childrens' jobs, family routines, living conditions (for example, how many people shared a bathroom? was it indoors or out of doors?), dinnertime rituals, division of labor inside and outside the home.

Small Group and Cooperative Projects (for older students): You might divide the class into groups to work on projects based on the information gathered for the heritage object. For example, illustrated timelines, or role-plays.

Art Projects: Students may present their own family story in creative form such as a story mural, collage, or poster.

Activity #3
FAMILY HERITAGE THROUGH LITERATURE:
A MESSAGE TO MY GRANDCHILD

Topic:	Personal history investigations through literature
Age:	8 and up
Concept:	There are patterns in family stories that make up a common history
Strategies:	• Personal History Investigations • Using Stories on the Same Theme • Creating Art • First Person Writing

Resources: There is a rich literature of family heritage stories. See bibliography for more suggested titles. These are some of our favorites: *Treasure Nap*, by J. Havill; *In Coal Country*, by J. Hendershot; *Grandfather's Journey*, by A. Say; *Peppe the Lamplighter*, by E. Bartone; *This Land is My Land*, by G. Littlechild; *The Sky was Blue*, by C. Zolotow; *The Always Prayer Shawl*, by S. Oberman; *My Place*, by N. Wheatley, D. Rawlins

Activity Profile: Students read different family heritage stories and compare elements of the story finding similarities and differences, such as: historical context, work, family life and problems, and migration. Students put themselves in the place of one of the characters. In the role of the character, they consider what they would want their great grandchild to know about their life. They create a picture or collage containing that message, and explain it in first person writing.

STEPS

Step 1. Read at least three different family heritage stories to the class. With each book, talk about the different cultural backgrounds and traditions represented in the story. Once personal connections are made in the first part of the learning spiral, ask students: (Questions will vary to suit the story)

- *When and where does the story take place? (find it on a map and locate it on a timeline)*
- *What work did people do? How is their work different from work today?*
- *What is family life like in the story? How is that different from today?*
- *What is life like for the child in the story?*
- *What problems do the characters in the story have? How do they solve them?*
- *Does anybody in the story move? If so, why? and from where to where?*
- *Does the book tell the story of a group of people?*
- *How does the author know this story?*

Step 2. As they read each story, compare all the questions across the stories. How are the answers similar and different for each story? Post questions and record students' ideas on large sheets of paper for later in the activity.

Step 3. Tell the students the following: All of the children in these stories lived in interesting times, some in times of great change. Some of these people changed the history of many generations because of things they did or decisions they made. In each story

46

there is a strong family or community or friend who helped the characters through tough times.

Ask students:

– *Which story would you like to be in? Which character would you want to be?*

Step 4. Tell students to put themselves in the place of the person they chose. Tell them to remember what they know about this character's work and family, problems and courage. For reminders, look at the book again, and look at the sheets made earlier in the activity. Ask:

– *What if you met your great grandchild?*
– *What would you like her to know about your life?*
– *What would you want her to remember and tell her grandchildren?*

Step 5. "Acting as if" they are the character they chose, students now draw a picture or make a collage of the things they would like a great grandchild to know. They draw themselves and their great grandchild in the middle of the picture.

They can frame the picture with a design or pattern which represents something special or important to the character.

Students then write their message for their grandchild, explaining what is in the picture and why it is important. The message can be written on a separate piece of paper or a "frame" may be made for the picture with the message written around the perimeter.

. . . .

CHAPTER FIVE

THROUGH OUR WORK

Perspective-taking activities

Introduction

> Do you still play in those bright fields? and are the flowers still there?
> There are no fields where I live now—no flowers anywhere!
> But day by day I go and turn a dull and tedious wheel:
> You cannot think how sad and tired and faint I often feel
>
> *from* Cheap Raw Material, *by M. Meltzer*[1]

Why is work an important topic in developing empathy and perspectives? As adults, most of our days are spent working. Work affects our lives profoundly. For some, it can provide satisfaction and an outlet for creativity; for others it may be mind-numbing and tedious. Work influences the amount of time we have for leisure and for family and friends. It affects the food we eat, the houses we live in, our ability to get an education, and our health. Through work, we gain access to some share of our society's resources.

Work also affects how people view us, and we them. People make judgments about others based on their occupations, often without knowing what it's like to do that kind of work, why they

48

do it, or what contribution their work makes. Assumptions often go unquestioned and prejudices are woven into the fabric of society. Our students pick up attitudes about workers from adults and media—attitudes that can affect children's feelings about themselves, as well as others.

In growing up, Kay Taus, one of the authors of *The Anti-Bias Curriculum* felt that her father's skills as a carpenter and television repairman were devalued. Now a teacher of young children, she writes, "I have children of very many different class backgrounds. I want to develop a respect for different kinds of work and an understanding that families have a variation in the lifestyle that they can afford."[2]

Because work has such a profound effect on our lives, learning about how different work situations shape people's experience of the world and their relationships to others is key to taking another's perspective . Understanding the perspectives of different workers helps students break down stereotypes and think critically about social issues, media images and their own role in society.

This chapter demonstrates ways to help students look through the eyes of different groups of workers now and in the past.

Although work is what most of us do much of the time, not many workers make it into the history books or onto the evening news broadcast. The work and daily lives of ordinary citizens today are rarely deemed newsworthy. And the adults and children who in the past labored up to sixteen hours a day on farms and railroads and in mills and factories did not write our history books.

If history records a myopic vision—that of the more successful or powerful members of society, can our students have an accurate picture of any historical period? Students ask "Who am I?" and "How am I connected to the past?" Can they piece together an answer without hearing the songs of everyday life sung by the man, woman or child leaving for work each dawn—songs which reveal why people may have moved, migrated, or fought to change circumstances and make unfair things more just?

The thoughts and feelings of women, the poorer classes and minorities can be discovered in a variety of sources: photographs, journals, oral histories, quilts and other art, historical fiction and biography. These sources tell tales of "how it was" for ordinary people—they tell of hard and important work, wretchedness, dreams, resiliency of spirit, and the will to overcome misfortune and pursue a better life. In this chapter, we use many of these sources to reveal the stories of workers around the world today and in the past.

History curricula can build on three connections between children and work:

- children are workers (most children in the world work)
- children use the products of work, and
- children come into contact with many different adult workers each day. Understanding the historical experience of workers and the value of their products and contributions builds a framework for respecting workers today.

In your class, a meaningful study of work and workers in other times and places starts with your students' own notions and understandings about work, and then expands beyond themselves to others. After investigating the role of work in their lives, they begin to ask questions about other children's lives. Are all children's lives simply spent in "school and play," as many of our students believe? Do they work? Has it historically been so? If children worked, when did they go to school or play with friends? How about children in other countries, or of other cultural or economic backgrounds?

This chapter presents four perspective-taking activities on work and workers in history, beginning with one entitled "Children at Work." Here students explore work through their own experience and through the eyes of child workers. Three other topics help students view daily life from the perspective of different workers in various historical and geographical settings: Chinese workers who built the United States and Canadian transcontinental railroads, women quilters around the world, and families working to make ends meet today. These are exemplars of lessons that you might teach about work in any period of your own country's history.

To help students explore the impact of work on people's lives, each of the lessons utilizes several perspective-taking strategies. "Wishes and Dreams" emphasizes one main part of the Thinking-Feeling Spiral: inquiring and imagining. "Children at Work," "The Snow Tiger" and "A Stitch in Time" demonstrate complete spirals. You may, however, choose to use any individual activity idea by itself. The strategy "Talking Photographs," for example, can be used with any historical topic or period.

Some of our examples are drawn from a United States context, but the activities can be adapted to your own curriculum. In some cases, you may choose to use our activities as presented, and then develop subsequent lessons specific to workers in your country. Alternatively, you may follow the activity sequence provided here, but substitute local stories, photos and secondary materials.

Activity # 1

CHILDREN AT WORK

Topic:	Child labor: work life of children in the early industrial labor force
Age:	8 and up
Concepts:	• Children work, in history and now • Changing unfair practices through child labor laws
Strategies:	• Photographs: "Talking Pictures" • Using Parallel Stories on the Same Theme • Visual Tools: Charts • Focusing on Critical Decision-Making Moments
Resources:	• Historical photographs by Lewis Hine • Biographical sketches of working children (Sources: M. Meltzer, *Cheap Raw Material*; R. Freedman, *Kids at Work: Lewis Hine and the Crusade Against Child Labor*)

Historical Background: In the process of industrialization, as people lost the ability to survive on family farms, families desperate to supplement their income often hired out their children to factories in developing urban areas. In the absence of protective child labor laws, these children were easily exploited, working twelve to sixteen hours a day for low pay, often in dangerous and unhealthy conditions.

In the United States, it was mostly the children of immigrants, particularly eastern European Jews and Italians, who ended up working in sweatshops. Fleeing pogroms and persecution in Russia and Poland, they sought refuge in America, the "land of opportunity," where they could live in freedom and work their way up.

The history of working children can be studied in any national context. This activity sequence may be used in studying a variety of topics including economic development, industrialization, and the migration of rural populations to cities and across national borders in search of work and freedom.

Activity Profile: Students will become aware of what kinds of work their peers and other children do now, and what work children did in the past. "Children at Work" highlights the use of historical photographs in helping students empathize with child workers, in this example, the ethnically diverse children whose labor fueled the United States economy prior to the passing of protective child labor laws. Through the photographs, students are asked to place themselves in other children's circumstances and think about how they would feel, and what life would be like. By reading biographies and eyewitness accounts, they move from thinking about one child in a photograph to finding out about many child workers in various occupations. Finally, they are asked to act as if they are members of a task force writing laws to protect children.

In extension projects, students apply their learning to current social problems. They learn that children all over the world today continue to work, many in sweatshop conditions where child labor laws are not practiced.

STEPS

Part One: *Making Personal Connections*

Option 1 (simpler)
Ask students what kind of work they and/or their siblings do at home or at after-school jobs. Lead a brief whole-group discussion. Why do they work? How do they feel about the work they do? Is there a legislated minimum wage? Does minimum wage vary with age? How much time do they spend working? Ask students whether they think most children in the world work. How might the work they do be the same or different? Have children worked throughout history?

Option 2 (more complex)
On the chalkboard, create a list of all the types of work students and their siblings do. Ask them how they might group the kinds of jobs they listed. Use colored chalk to color-code which jobs belong together. After the jobs are grouped in categories, find out how many students do each type of work. Ask how much time they spend at each kind of task. What patterns do they see in the data? How many classmates or siblings work? What kinds of work do they do? How much time do they spend working? Now ask how this might be the same or different for other children around the

world. Have children worked throughout history? Elicit questions about other children's work.

Part Two: *Imagining and Inquiring Using Talking Photographs*

Talking photographs may be done alone as a separate activity, or with the other parts.

Step 1. Select historical photos of children doing different kinds of work. Here, we use Lewis Hine's photographs of early twentieth century United States industries: breaker boys in the coal mines and cannery workers.

You may wish to create overheads from the photos or from this book so that you can project them at the front of the room.

"Cannery Workers Preparing Beans, 1910" by Lewis Hine, Courtesy of Library of Congress

"Young West Virginia Coal Miner" by Lewis Hine, Courtesy of Library of Congress

Step 2. Display a photo. Select some of the questions from the Photo Question Set below to ask the students. You are now modeling with the whole group the task students will soon do in Step 4 as they investigate a second photograph with a partner.

Photo Question Set

- *Who are these children? What do you think they are doing?*
- *What do you think these children are thinking or feeling? How do you know? (Probes: What do their faces tell us? What does their clothing tell us?)*
- *What do you think they would say to you if they could talk? What might they say to one another? What language would they be speaking?*
- *What are the objects in the photo? What are they used for? Who uses them? For how long, do you think? To whom do they belong?*
- *When do you think these photos were taken? How do you know? Where might they have been taken?*
- *Sensory: As someone in the picture, what would you smell? hear? taste?*
- *What do you think happened before the picture was taken?*
- *Imagine that the people started moving and speaking as if in a film. What would they do?*
- *Imagine you are small enough to hide in this photo. Where would you hide? What would you see from your hiding place?*
- *If you could walk through the landscape in this photograph, what shoes would you wear? Describe where you would start your walk, and what you would see as you walk.*
- *What is the photographer trying to say?*

Step 3. Team each student with a partner or form small groups. Give each group or partner team a different photograph of children working.

Step 4. Referring to their photograph, ask students to discuss and record their answers to selected questions from the Photo Question Set.

Step 5. After all partner teams have finished, ask volunteers to hold up their photographs and discuss their responses to the questions.

Step 6. To conclude this activity sequence, ask students how these children's lives are like or unlike their own lives. Refer back to the initial discussion of work done by students in the class. Discuss whether they would have liked to have been a child at the turn of the century. What do they now wonder about children who worked then? Generate a list of questions (these may become research topics or questions that guide further reading of fiction or non-fiction).

You may choose to conclude the activity at this point, or go on...

Part Three: *Charting Patterns and Comparisons*

Step 1. Divide students into small cooperative work groups of approximately five students each. Give each group a different brief narrative sheet (examples included) about children working at various jobs and a copy of the Child Work Data Sheet.

Step 2. Tell groups to fill out the Child Work Data Sheet for the child in their narrative. They will need to ponder and discuss the last question, "How did your child feel about this work?" Tell them to think about how they might feel in similar circumstances.

Child Work Data Sheet

Age	Hours of Work
Why they work	
Kind of work	
Effect on education	
Health hazards	
How the worker feels	

Step 3. Make a large class Child Work Data Chart on the chalkboard. Compile the information about *all* the child workers as each group reports.

Step 4. Ask the class what pattern they see for each category. For example, how old were the child workers? (All were under twelve years of age.) How long did they work? (All worked at least twelve hours a day.) What statement can we make about why they worked?

You may choose to conclude the activity at this point, or go on...

Part Four: *"Acting As If . . ."*

Step 1. Group students as in Part Three. Explain: It is the early 1900s, and your group has been elected to the National Child Labor Committee. You must investigate the conditions of work for children, determine what kind of protection these children need, and decide what actions the government should take to protect child workers.

Step 2. Each group lists:

- how children are being treated unfairly
- what protections they need
- what child labor laws should be created

Step 3. Report your committee's recommendations.

Part Five: *Optional Extension Projects*

1. **Personal History Investigation.** What kind of work did our grandparents and great-grandparents do when they were young? What were their working conditions? Develop a question list for interviewing an older generation about work. Compile information on a class chart similar to the Child Work Data Chart.

2. **Current Social Issues.** Compare children's work in the early twentieth century to children's work today. An on-line source may provide news articles/pictures about a variety of working children around the world (for example, child carpet workers in India). In groups, ask students to construct a Venn Diagram comparing lives of child workers in the early 1900s to the children in the news articles. They may also compare child labor laws in different countries.

3. **Connecting to Children's Literature:** Read a piece of historical fiction about a child laborer, for example, Katherine Paterson's

Lyddie. Compare the character's life to what students learned from their photographs and research.

Activity #2

THE SNOW TIGER:
MOVING MOUNTAINS TO BUILD THE RAILROAD

Topic:	Chinese workers and the building of the railroads
Age:	10 and up
Concepts:	• The labor of many groups of people built our countries • Immigrant workers often experience prejudice. They may work at oppressive, dangerous and poorly paid tasks • People have acted in history to change unfair conditions
Strategies:	• Combining Secondary Sources with Children's Fiction • First Person Journals • A Pattern of Questions
Resources:	• Historical fiction: L. Yep, *Dragon's Gate* • Non-fiction sources: R. Blumberg, *Full Steam Ahead* and R. Takaki, *Journey to Gold Mountain*

Activity Profile: This activity demonstrates how to create rich first person journals using fiction combined with secondary sources. Choose a compelling piece of contemporary or historical fiction through which students can identify with a character from another time or place. To provide detailed information, students read one or more non-fiction sources alongside the fiction. As they read in small or large groups, they discuss questions that help them move from thinking about their own lives to thinking about the life of the fictional character and from his story to the story of many others like him.

Prejudice and hardship faced by immigrant workers is a global theme. In this example from the book *Dragon's Gate*, students investigate conditions faced by Chinese and Irish railroad workers as they dig a tunnel through almost impenetrable rock. They probe inequalities in compensation paid to Chinese and Irish workers, and keep a journal from the viewpoint of Otter, a fourteen-year-old Chinese boy as he comes to terms with the discrepancies between dreams and realities in his new country. The activity sequence may be applied to immigrant groups in other contexts, using appropriate children's fiction and secondary sources.

Historical Background: In the late nineteenth century, turmoil in China provided the impetus for people to leave the country in large numbers. Many Chinese men were drawn to Canada and the United States because of the need for railroad workers to build the transcontinental railroads. Chinese workers on the Canadian Pacific Railway carved roads for track in the mountainous gorges of British Columbia. At one point, 90% of the workers on the Central Pacific Railroad were Chinese. For years, Chinese and Irish workers labored under dangerous and oppressive mountain and desert conditions. They worked long hours for low pay through great hardships; it is estimated that 1200 Chinese railroad workers died in the United States during this time.

Dragon's Gate is told through the eyes of Otter, a fourteen-year-old boy who is born in China's Kwantung Province. Otter joins his father and uncle in the Sierra Mountains, where he confronts inequality and disappointment as part of a work crew. Through Otter's eyes, the reader learns about life in the forbidding worksite which the Chinese called The Snow Tiger.

STEPS

Step 1. Identify key social issues that impact the character's life and key passages or chapters where they are discussed in the fiction.

In *Dragon's Gate* these issues might be:
    Cross cultural relationships (Otter's friendship with Sean,
    the Irish boy)
    Daily life in camp (hardships, survival, entertainment)
    Inequalities in work conditions (Chinese and Irish)
    The strike (a key decision-making moment)

Step 2. For each key issue, use the pattern of questions to help students make personal connections and to imagine and inquire about the main character. As students read a chapter of *Dragon's Gate* that highlights one of the key issues, stop and discuss the questions in a large group or small groups. Have students take notes they may refer to when writing their journals later.

Dragon's Gate Question Set

- Otter's Friendship with Sean, an Irish boy
  - *Did you ever have a friendship with someone very different from you? How did you first meet? What did your parents think about your friendship?*
  - *What was Sean and Otter's first meeting like? How did Otter's and Sean's parents react to their friendship?*
  - *What do you think parents worry about when kids make friends?*
  - *Why did you value your friendship? Why do you think Otter valued his friendship with Sean?*

- Daily Life in the Work Camp
  - *Have you ever been in a situation where survival was difficult or known someone who has?*
  - *What was it like? How did you keep warm? Get food? Protect yourself from the weather?*
  - *How was it different from your daily life now?*
  - *Have you ever been in a situation without technology, television, telephones, toilets, running water or separate houses? What would be different about your everyday life under these circumstances?*
  - *What was the food like in Otter's work camp? How does this compare to your food?*
  - *What were the rooms like? Describe or draw the surroundings.*
  - *List the items that Otter needed for survival in the camp.*

- Unequal Working Conditions for Chinese and Irish
  - *Have you ever been in a situation where you felt you worked harder than someone else? Have you ever felt unfairly treated? Describe the circumstances.*
  - *What work conditions did both the Irish and Chinese have to endure in the railroad work camps? How were they treated differently?*

- The Strike
  - *What do you know about strikes? Has anyone you know ever participated in a strike?*
  - *Have you ever tried to change something that was unfair to make it fair? How did you do it? What happened?*
  - *What were some of Otter's issues and feelings around the strike?*

Step 3. Now have students consider: is this character's experience typical? Is what happened to Otter similar to what happened to other Chinese immigrant workers? Ask students to consider what might be fact or fiction in the book. To answer this question, have students read excerpts from primary or secondary sources about Chinese railroad workers. They can then compare Otter's story with the non-fiction sources.

The chart below shows one way for notes to be organized:

Notes from Fiction: *Dragon's Gate*	Notes from Other historical sources
Cross-cultural friendship: The friendship of Sean and Otter *How did they meet? What did they think of each other? How did they communicate? What was difficult? What did they value about each other? How did they help each other? What conflicts did they have?*	**Cross-cultural friendship: Irish workers and Chinese workers on the railroads** same questions
Daily life at the Snow Tiger camps: hardships and survival *What was the food like? Where and how did they live? How did they try to stay clean, healthy and warm? What was different for the Chinese and the Irish? Did they see things the same way? How did they entertain themselves? How did they protect themselves?*	**Daily life in other camps: hardships and survival** same questions
Unequal working conditions, unfair practices *What work conditions (pay, safety, hours, penalties) did the Chinese and the Irish endure? How were they treated differently from other workers? What practices do you think were unfair?*	**Unequal working conditions, unfair practices in other camps** same questions
The strike *What were issues and feelings about the strike? Why did the Chinese want to strike? Why were they afraid to strike? Why do you think Otter did what he did?*	**Strikes** *Were there strikes? What were they about? Why did they want to strike/not want to strike?*

Step 4. Now students write a first person journal "acting as if" they were Otter. Begin by saying, "Imagine that you can step into the shoes of Otter. Instead of being yourself, you *are* Otter. Write journal entries in his words. Use your notes to fill your journal with the details that will make your entry convincing." Student journals may be about one or more of the key issues for Otter. For example, journal prompts might be:

- *How do you feel about your friendship with Sean, and how has it changed?*
- *What is your daily life in camp like and what do you think and feel about it?*
- *What do you think is unfair about how you and your crew are treated?*
- *Pretend you are Otter making a decision about the strike. Would you strike or not?*

The whole process of writing journals using fiction and non-fiction sources looks like this:

Note: You can create the environment that helps students imagine being Otter by posting photographs from those times or playing folk songs from the groups represented in the book.

Activity # 3

A STITCH IN TIME:
WOMEN QUILTING

A quilt won't forget. It can tell your life story.

from The Patchwork Quilt, *by Valerie Flournoy*[3]

Quilts are the stories of our lives. They tell the history of our families and communities. They are expressions of our love, hopes, hard work and patience in the face of what life hands us. That's what piecing is.

Topics:
- Traditional work of women across cultures
- Cultural history preserved through quilts

Age: 8–14

Concepts:
- Women's work is critical in history
- Quilts become cherished reflections of time, place and culture
- Women have traditionally created quilts and weaving in different cultures and times in history

Strategies:
- Children's Literature: Parallel Stories on the Same Theme
- A Pattern of Questions
- First Person Writing and Dramatizing

Resources:
- Picture books of quilt stories. Suggested titles: P. Polacco, *The Keeping Quilt*; V. Flournoy, *The Patchwork Quilt*; T. Johnston & T. DePaola, *The Quilt Story*; O. Castaneda, *Abuela's Weave*; G. Guback, *Luka's Quilt*; E. Coerr, *The Josefina Story Quilt*
- Optional: Non-fiction books about quilts
- Quiltmaking Object Box containing such items as: needles, thread, variety of fabrics, batting, hoop, etc.
- Demonstration quilts made of paper or fabric

Historical Background: Around the world, women have pieced, woven, and sewn beautiful quilts and coverings for their families and also as a means of income. Sometimes called "heart work," quilts and other textile arts are rich reflections of cultural and personal aesthetics. The variety of stitches, patterns and colors in textile art is unlimited. Quilts have been traced to the earliest beginnings of civilization in Northern Africa, the Middle East, and India. They reached Europe two thousand years later, worn by Crusaders returning from the Middle East. Before long, quilting was known as a highly useful and expressive form of needlework practiced by women across economic classes and cultures. In North America, quilting found new inspirations as necessity and cultural influences combined to simultaneously retain and transform the traditional craft. The patchwork quilt emerged from the hardships of daily life, as scraps of fabric were saved and sewn together to perform yet another job, to keep a child warm and to serve as a reminder of past deeds, adventures, and even cultural beliefs. Today, handmade quilts are used as blankets or are displayed as decorative art. They are still handed down from generation to generation, and are often vehicles for warm retelling of family stories.

Activity Profile: This activity demonstrates the use of parallel stories on the same theme to explore patterns in history. Our theme here is women's work as quilters. Similar activities can be designed using literature on a variety of other themes, following the same sequence, or using part of the sequence. Here, students read a selection of picture books about a cherished family quilt or weaving. In each story, the quilt bonds the family together, creating a sense of continuity and security, especially between the girls and women of different generations. Using the pattern of questions as well as mind maps and charts, students find similarities and differences among the stories. Each student then chooses to "become" a particular quilter, and writes a short piece entitled "Why I Made the Quilt" from that quilter's perspective. Finally, with the help of a "time machine," all the "quilters" come together for a dramatized exhibit and presentation in a "local museum."

STEPS

Step 1. Before reading any of the books, ask questions to create personal and concrete connections between students and the idea of quilts.

> – *Have you ever made something by hand and given it to another person?*

– Were you ever given something that someone else made for you?

– Do you have a quilt or other hand-made item? Who gave it to you? Who made it?

– What does it feel like to wrap up in a quilt?

Step 2. Show some pictures of quilts (see bibliography) or bring in a real quilt for the students to look at, feel and ask questions about. Look at the colors, textures, stitchery, shapes, patterns, etc.

– What do you see?

– How do you think it was made?

– What do you think it would be like to make a quilt?

Step 3. Read one of the picture books to the class. In each of the quilt stories chosen for this activity, the quilt helps the young character to remember or learn something about her family. The character experiences a transformation having to do with cultural identity, strengthened relationships, responsibility, or growing up. For example, in *Luka's Quilt*, Luka, a Hawaiian girl, at first rejects the quilt her grandmother makes for her because it is not colorful, as she had expected:

> *"This is the way we make our quilts," said Tutu. "Two colors. It's our Island tradition. You chose green, remember?"*
> *"I thought the green was for leaves," I cried. "All the flowers in our garden are in colors. It can't be a flower garden if the flowers are white."*
> *Tutu's eyes got watery, and she quietly turned and went to her room and shut the door.*
> *I looked at Tutu's quilt again. I thought it was going to be so pretty, and all it was white. I sat down and cried."*
> from *Luka's Quilt*, by Georgia Guback

Step 4. Using a large piece of stiff paper that can be saved, create a **mind map** to identify and organize aspects of the story. The mind map focuses on the significance of the quilt in the lives of the characters, how it strengthened their relationships, and how it helped them "remember." This mind map will be the model for mind-mapping the other quilt stories.

Your mind map might look like this:

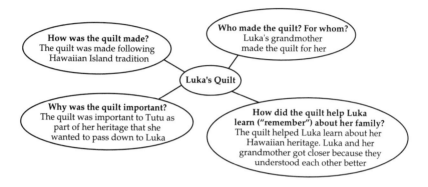

Step 5. Read several other stories in small groups, assigning one story to each group. Each group makes a mind map following the steps that you modeled with the whole class, as in the example above. Alternatively, read and mind-map each book with the whole class.

Step 6. After all the stories have been read, post the mind maps. Ask the class to look for patterns in the stories. Help your students move from the particulars of each story to the general patterns that emerge across stories by emphasizing the quilts, quilters, generations of women, etc.

— *What patterns do we see? What did the quilters in the stories have in common?*
— *How were each of these quilts used to help the families remember? What were they remembering? How can a quilt help someone remember?*
— *What did the quilter do to make the quilt a way to tell the family story?*
— *What do you think it was like for the children in the stories to help make and to receive the quilts?*

Step 7. As students begin to see commonalities and differences, make a simple chart like the one below to show these patterns.

Book Title	Who made the quilt? Who was the quilt for?	How did the different generations see and do things differently?	How does the quilt "help remember?" Does it help change someone?
Luka's Quilt (Hawaiian)	Tutu (Luka's grand mother) made the quilt for Luka.	Luka didn't like the color. Tutu's feelings were hurt. They compromised. Tutu made a colorful lei to add to the quilt	Luka's quilt helped her learn about her Hawaiian heritage, and how important it was to her grandmother to pass on the quilting tradition.
The Patchwork Quilt (African American)	Grandmother made the quilt for Tanya.	Grandmother got sick and couldn't work on the quilt. Tanya helped finish the quilt. Tanya's mother helped make the quilt, too.	The quilt was made of fabrics from special clothes and from events. It taught Tanya about traditional quilting and would help her remember her Grandmother's love for her family. It brought her closer to her mother.
Abuela's Weave (Guatemalan)			

Step 8. Tell students that each of them is going to pretend to be one of the quilters. Each of them has received an invitation from their town's museum to share his or her quilt and tell the story that goes with it. They are going to write their stories, entitled "Why I made the quilt," in the first person. Help them get into their role by surrounding them with quilts, sewing supplies, and pictures. Instruct them to look at their mind maps for details of their quilting experience, including where, when, why, and how they made their quilt. Their stories should include the following information:

– *Why did you decide to make the quilt?*
– *Where were you when you made it? When did you make it?*
– *Who did you make it for?*
– *What kind of fabric did you use? Where did you get it?*
– *Did something important happen while you were making the quilt?*
– *What did the quilt mean to you?*
– *Are you pleased with the way the story of your quilt has worked out?*

Step 9. Each student writes the story of "Why I made the quilt" and shares it with the class.

Optional: Students may want to create demonstration quilts made of paper, paint or fabric, or create other visual aids. Your class may stage a mock mini-museum exhibit and presentation. This can be performed for your class only, or for other classes invited to your "Museum Quilt Show."

Activity #4

WISHES AND DREAMS

Topic:	Work and family resources; families' wishes around the world
Age:	8–12
Concepts:	• All families work to meet their needs and pursue their dreams for the future. • There are vast differences in the distribution of material wealth among peoples of the world
Strategies:	• Creating Art: Imagine and draw • First Person Writing
Resources:	• Magazine pictures of different kinds of work and a range of life circumstances • P. Menzel, *Material World: A Global Family Portrait*

Activity Profile: In this activity, students explore differences in work and wealth among families around the world. They begin by looking at magazine pictures that show different kinds of work. Through questioning and discussion, they think about differences in families' work situations and access to material resources. They then read a series of "wishes for the future" from families around the world. They hypothesize about daily life in various families. Using their imaginations, they draw and write in the first person about one family's wishes for the future.

If available, you can use the book *Material World* by P. Menzel, which shows thirty families around the world who agreed to be photographed with all their material possessions in front of their homes. The compelling portraits of these families illuminate vast discrepancies linked to the distribution of land and resources, access to education and jobs, and per capita income. Students see a variety of work arrangements. In some photographs all family members work together on the land or in small family owned enterprises; in others, members of the family earn wages away from the home. Some live and work in cities; some in rural areas.

STEPS:

Step 1. Set the stage using *Material World* or magazine pictures that show people working around the world. Include a variety of ways people make a living, with a range of compensations. Ask:

– *What kinds of work do you see in these pictures?*
– *Is it like the work that your family does? Who do you think the people are?*
– *What are the objects in the pictures? What are they used for?*
– *What resources does the family in the picture have?*
– *What kind of compensation do you think they get for their work? What makes you think so?*
– *What necessities and other items do you think the family has?*

Explain that within any one country there are differences in the resources families have, and people do different kinds of work to provide for their families' needs and wants. Some people work in their houses or on the land. In many families, everyone works. Some families grow food and make some of their own clothing. Many others earn money to buy food and clothing. Some people move to cities to find work. Some do not earn enough money to meet their families' needs or to buy things they would like to have.

To begin modeling the activity, discuss the following ideas: "All families have wishes for the future. Our wishes are often tied to what we think we need to make our lives better. If my family lives in a dry climate and we grow our own food, we may wish for a water system. If my family lives in a city where transportation to a job is important, we may wish for the car to be repaired, or for a new car." Display and discuss the "Wishes List" shown below from families around the world.

1. Irrigation system, enclosed garden, motorcycle
2. More animals, second set of clothes, better seed stock, farm implements, peace in area and world
3. A permanent house for all seasons made of wood and cement with a corrugated iron roof. A garden inside the fence.
4. TV with 30" screen, VCR, refrigerator, more tools, drugs to combat diseases in fish breeding
5. 1 or 2 new cows for milk
6. Stereo, color TV, automobile (all to be financed by sale of rice field adjacent to house)
7. Tools, new carpet, camping trailer
8. Truck
9. New refrigerator, house in country, cleaner environment
10. Fishing boat, more income and leisure time for vacations
11. To have one (a future), if so, then a VCR, camera, more income

Step 2. Choosing one example from the Wishes List in Step 1, ask students why they think someone would make that wish. Ask:

— *What kind of work do you think the family who wished for this does?*
— *Who in the family do you think works?*
— *How do they get the things they need to live—food, clothing, shelter, money?*
— *Imagine the family in front of their house. What would the house be like?*
— *What could you say about the family's daily life?*
— *How might you show the family's work and wishes in a drawing?*

Step 3 (Drawing and Writing). Pair students. Give each pair one of the wishes from the Wishes List. Partners read their wish and try to answer the questions listed in Step 2 for the family who made this wish. They then:

1. draw a portrait of the family, showing where they live and something about their work
2. imagine they are a member of that family and write a few sentences about their daily life.

Here's one student's drawing of wishes for an irrigation system and an enclosed garden.

My family lives on a farm. We have one cow and that's how we get our milk. The cow eats grass. The grass needs water but we don't have a lot of rain. We want to grow more food and sell some at the market. The animals eat our garden so we need a fence and more water. We need a way to get to town five miles away. If we had a motorcycle, we could go to town and I could get to school. Here is my mom, dad, brothers, me and our animals.

Step 4. Post all the drawings. Have students guess where each of the families live (rural/urban? which part of the world?) and what kind of work they do. How do they know? What resources do they think the family has?

What did you learn about what people wish for? How is it related to what they need and have? What assumptions did you make when you drew your pictures?

As a follow-up, research information about work and resources in the countries the wishes came from. You may want students to graph and compare data about the distribution of wealth and resources around the world. What patterns do they see in the data and why they think the distribution of resources is so unequal?

COUNTRIES LIST

1. Mali
2. Ethiopia
3. Mongolia
4. China
5. India
6. Thailand

7. United States
8. Mexico
9. Germany
10. Kuwait
11. Israel

. . . .

CHAPTER SIX

THROUGH OUR MIGRATIONS

Perspective-taking activities

Introduction

> "There wasn't enough food where we used to live."
> "We moved so no one would bother us when we went to church."
> "There were tanks in the street outside our house. I was scared."
> "The police were putting everybody in jail."
>
> *from* Coming To America *by D. Fassler & K. Danforth*[4]

The above quotes capture the real experience of children whose families have moved across borders in search of economic opportunity or to escape poverty, war or oppression. Pushed by desperation and lured by dreams, "immigrants are changing the face of nations and often experiencing an angry backlash in some of them."[5]

Our communities and our classrooms reflect the movements of peoples across and within national borders. Our students come from all over the world. Some have moved many, many times in their young lives; some can trace their ancestry back to one country or neighborhood over many generations. But their families, too, once migrated and carry with them the collective memory of other places.

As one teacher, Teresa, put it,

My students come from all around the world. The details of their lives are often shocking, and I find it difficult to imagine their past circumstances and how they had the courage to overcome them. How can my other students understand — when their lives have been so different? Many grew up on the same street; even in the same house. Some have never been out of their neighborhood. Their languages are different. What is the common ground in their experience? How can I, as a teacher, help them see the world through each other's eyes?

Another teacher spoke of a Vietnamese child who movingly told her how much she missed her grandfather playing the cello and how sad she was that she would not hear it again. Her story reminds us that memories are always a mixture of sadness and joy, and that what families leave behind in their country of origin is dear to them.

When people migrate, they help to change the identity of the communities and nations in which they live. But these changes are not often reflected in the local curriculum. Teresa helps her students understand each other by making their stories an explicit focus of her social studies. We believe, as she does, that those who have experienced the hardships and hopes of migration, should find people like themselves in the local and national history they study. We learn that all peoples migrated once, as part of other voluntary or forced historical waves of migration. Studying migration stories, we can see that some of our peers, parents and grandparents have been through similar experiences. We can come to understand the feelings of people who have had to move, and admire their determination and strength. Thus all students—those for whom migration has only a distant meaning, as well as those who are newcomers—can empathize and inquire about their world through different eyes.

As teachers, we want our students to identify that *core of common experience* that enables them to see themselves reflected in another. This helps them to reject dehumanizing stereotypes, to respect the dignity of all people and to rejoice in our possibilities. As Sybella Wilkes noted,

Refugees are people just like you and me who, through no fault of their own have been caught up in major upheavals. They are doctors and

lawyers, farmers and fishermen, mothers, fathers and children. Albert Einstein and Sigmund Freud were refugees. What if the world had turned its back on them?" [(6)]

In this chapter, we help students explore together what it is like to leave home and struggle to survive in a new land. Why do people move? What do they encounter when they do move? How do children in the sending and receiving communities learn about one another, form friendships, and deal with fears or animosities? How do our actions and reactions affect the immigrant children with whom we work and play? The answers to these questions are essential in developing trust, empathy and community in the classroom.

People migrate for many different reasons. Some leave voluntarily, drawn to other countries by economic opportunity; some are driven out by oppression, war or famine; some are forced by the military to relocate as a result of specific government edicts. The activities in this chapter reflect these voluntary and involuntary migration experiences, historical and contemporary, across borders and within borders.

Half of all today's refugees are children. We use their real stories because their own words are powerful testimonies to the migration experience for other children. Using examples from Southeast Asia, Eastern Europe, Africa and Central America, the first two activities, "The Buddha Statue" and "Story Cloths," help students reconstruct the circumstances that drive people from their homeland, the choices people face and the obstacles they must overcome. Through writing and art, students walk in the shoes of migrating families, making decisions and chronicling the joys, sorrows and feats of their journeys.

The third activity, "The Trail of Tears," focuses on a historical instance of forced migration: the removal of the Cherokee people from their homeland. Here students investigate the devastating effect of migration policy on human lives and why migration policy is often the center of tremendous conflict. Migrant workers play an important part in economies all over the world. In "Radio Message Center," students look through the eyes of children of migrant workers as they learn what it's like to leave relatives and friends when families relocate for work. The last activity, "Snapshots of Life in My New Country," provides students with opportunities to solve problems faced by recent immigrants to their own schools and communities.

As in Chapter 5 in "Children at Work", each of the perspective-taking activities in this chapter utilizes several strategies in a Thinking-Feeling Spiral. Each serves as a prototype for activities you may design with migration topics in your own context. Although we present activity sequences, you may use any segment by itself. Please be aware that the activities in this unit need to be handled very sensitively (or modified) if your class includes children who have suffered traumatic relocations.

Activity #1

THE BUDDHA STATUE

Topic:	Migration, refugees, Southeast Asian history
Age:	10 and up
Concepts:	• Why people emigrate • What happens to refugees? How we know their stories
Strategies:	• Primary Sources • "What-If...?" Writing • A Pattern of Questions
Resources:	• "The Buddha Statue" (story included) • Cambodia Information Sheet • Students' own stories of their families' migrations can be used

Historical Background: The 1960s began a period of three decades of dislocation and terror for millions of Cambodians. Civil war, war with Vietnam, United States bombing aimed at communist base camps, crop destruction and famine all contributed to homelessness and the flight of millions of Cambodians to refugee camps.

Around the world today, natural and man-made disasters, including devastating civil wars, are creating situations which force people to leave their homes. There are today 19 million refugees; over half of these are children.

Activity Profile: This is an inquiry-based activity. Beginning with a child's account of her family's escape from war-torn Cambodia, the teacher asks a set of connecting and imagining questions. Students develop a stake in discovering the circumstances of the story—what that war was about, what happened to civilians, why people tried to escape, how it might have been possible for refugees

74

to survive in Thailand. Students become the historians, generating their own questions and developing hypotheses. Once invested in the fate of the storyteller, students are given a brief historical information sheet about Cambodia and Cambodian refugees. Placing themselves in the circumstances of the story, they must decide what they will do. Then they write the next chapter.

This activity can be adapted to a study of refugees and migration around the world. Any first-person account can be used with a similar questioning sequence and writing activity.

The Buddha Statue

(Story written by an eleven-year-old refugee)

The Buddha statue was found in the field of corn in the year of 1977. In that time there was a war. My dad found the statue when he was working for the soldiers at night. He didn't know what it was. But he knew it was a rock that was carved and it was very interesting. So he put it in his pocket when it was time to go home at 12:00 a.m. Then he fell asleep with nothing in his mind. Not even the statue.

There were 20 people in our little cramped cottage. And the worst of all was there were four different families in the same cottage.

The next morning, he woke everyone up and the first thing my dad did was take the statue from his pocket and show them. Everyone saw it and was puzzled. They were still talking about the Buddha statue at 5:00 a.m. And they have be at work at 4:30. So they were late for work. In a few minutes, the soldiers came and knocked on the door. My mom hurried and hid the statue. A boy pretended to be sick. When the soldiers came in a lady lied, "We didn't go to work because we're worried about him, sir."

That night after work they all started to pray to the Buddha statue and hope we could escape.

The next morning the soldiers from the other side had started shooting and bombing. All the people in our cottage escaped from the bombing and shooting. The people from the other cottages had tried to escape, but most died. My family believed that it was the Buddha's power that helped them escape from the war.

We crossed the border to Thailand. They were shooting over there too. But we made it.

Part One: *Buddha Story Questions and Responses*

Step 1. Read the story aloud and give copies to students in partners. Ask the students:

– *What do you think this story is about?*
– *How do you think the families in the cottage felt?*
– *Have you ever felt this way?*
– *Is this story like any other you know?*

Step 2. Ask students to draw a picture of what they think is happening in one part of the story. Include as much detail as they can find in the story. At the bottom of the picture, write their feelings about what they think is happening.

Step 3. Ask each set of partners to reread the story and make up two questions. As the class discusses the questions, use the list below to pose questions not mentioned by the students.

– *Where are the people in the story? (what are some clues? Refer to a map)*
– *Who do you think the soldiers could be?*
– *Who do you think is telling the story?*
– *Why do you think there are so many people in the cottage?*
– *Why are they working at night? What are they doing?*
– *How long do they work each day/night?*
– *Why do you think the statue was buried? How did it get there?*
– *How do you think they escaped?*
– *Why do you think the Buddha statue was so important to them? How did it "save them?"*
– *Have you ever felt protected like this?*
– *Do you think this family had a choice about leaving their country?*

Step 4. After students have shared their questions and possible responses, distribute the Cambodia Information Sheet and information on refugees. Supplement with other resources. Ask them to read with their partner and jot down any further answers they can discover. Then revisit the questions as a whole class.

CAMBODIA INFORMATION SHEET

What caused the fighting in the 1970s?

- a group called the Khmer Rouge, led by Pol Pot, wanted to rid the country of anyone who did not support its policies
- city people were sent to the countryside to do forced labor
- families were broken up
- religion was brutally suppressed. Buddhist temples were destroyed and people arrested, tortured and killed
- destruction was caused by American bombs trying to destroy communist camps in Cambodia
- beginning in 1978, fighting between Pol Pot's army and the invading Vietnamese army destroyed much of the rice harvest and created a famine
- of Cambodia's 1975 population of seven million, about one million died from assassination, malnutrition or forced labor

What happened to the refugees from Cambodia?

- Large numbers of Cambodians fled the fighting into Thailand between 1975 and 1982
- refugees spent months and even years in the refugee camps in Thailand, Malaysia, Hong Kong, Guam or the Philippines before some of them were allowed to enter the United States, Canada or other countries
- Conditions in the refugee camps varied enormously. Some had adequate supplies of food and medicine and some schooling and English-language instruction for those going to America. Other camps had substandard food and housing, no educational programs, and little or no protection against criminals and reprisal raids from across the border.

> — Paula Gillett, "Cambodian Refugees:
> An Introduction to their History and Culture" in
> Karen Jorgensen-Esmaili, *New Faces of Liberty*.[7]

77

Refugee Information

In a United Nations High Commissioner Refugee camp, people are given protection from physical harm and from being forced to return to their own land. They are given relief assistance such as food, water, shelter and medical care. However, resources are scarce. You can get into a camp if you are classified as a refugee.

"A refugee is someone who has fled across a national border from his or her home country, or is unable to return to it because of a well-founded fear that he or she will be persecuted for reasons of race, religion, nationality or political opinion. Refugees who cross borders because of famine are not necessarily covered by international protection, unlike refugees fleeing from war and so on."[8]

A refugee camp is a place you cannot leave without authorization.

Part Two: *"What If. . . ?" Writing.*

Step 1. "The Buddha Statue" is a "story without an end." The narrator stops at the Thai border. Ask students to pretend they are the person who wrote "The Buddha Statue." Each set of partners is going to write and illustrate the next chapter. Their story will be written in the first person.

Step 2. To get students thinking, together make a list of problems a refugee family coming across a border might have to solve. Here are some suggestions to supplement the students' list:

– *What happened when your family got across the Thai border?*
– *Where could you go to live in Thailand?*
– *How could you manage to get food and shelter?*
– *Who might help you? Do you know anyone?*
– *What resources can you rely on? What work can you do?*
– *How can you get to a refugee camp? What is life like in the refugee camp? Whom do you meet?*
– *How can you try to improve life in the camp?*
– *How can you eventually leave the refugee camp? Where might you go? To what country?*
– *What would you try to do to improve life in the meantime?*

Step 3. In writing their story chapter, students may choose one or more of the writing prompts below. Before writing, have partners choose whether they will write about when "crossing the border" or what they will do "at the refugee camp." Then have them discuss which course of action they would take if they were in the story and why.

- Writing Prompts

"When you first cross the border"

- Find someone connected with the government (a police officer or government official). Tell him you are being persecuted in Cambodia. If you return to your country, you are afraid you will be hurt or killed.
- Find a church or temple and ask for protection. Find someone who speaks both your language and the language of the new country. Or, describe how you will communicate without knowing the Thai language. Explain what you need and how you might get help.
- Trade your skills for food. From the story, what kind of skills do you know you have that you might be able to trade for food and shelter? Remember, too, that many Cambodian families moved to the countryside from the cities before the story took place. What work might you have done in the cities?

"At the refugee camp"

There are 70,000 people in your United Nations High Commissioner camp on the Thai-Cambodian border. The camp does not have enough resources to meet the needs of the people who live there.

- If there is land, find ways to get seeds so you won't go hungry. Perhaps talk to someone in the camp who may trade seeds. If you have a fruit or vegetable, plant the seeds from it. What else will help improve your family's diet?
- Most people are living in bamboo and thatched huts. More people need houses. Many children in the camp cannot read or write in Khmer (their own language) because they have been homeless and without schools

for many years. You can organize a camp team to teach, build classrooms or houses, or make teaching materials (there are no books). Describe what might be needed and how you might go about doing this.

- Find a way to get to the local town where you might find salespeople, journalists, photographers, medical personnel, tourists, scholars and volunteers. Can any of them help you?
- Apply to go to Canada, France, the United States, or Australia. How will you decide which country to go to? Not everyone can go. If too many people apply to a country, you may have to break up your family. Who will go and who will stay? How will you feel? Whoever goes will need to learn to speak English or French and have some contacts in your new country. Can anyone in the camp help you?
- The United Nations runs a resettlement program, allowing you to volunteer to return to Cambodia when things are more peaceful. You may choose to return to any village where you have relatives; or, small groups of families from the camp may go together to a United Nations "receiving site." If you volunteer to return, the United Nations will provide mosquito nets, temporary shelter, seeds, agricultural tools, carpentry kits, one medical kit and about $80 to start out with. However, you don't know what the situation will be like in your country. What are you worried about?

Step 4. After students share their stories, conclude by discussing the following:

- *What did we learn about why people migrate?*
- *What did we learn about what it's like to uproot and try to resettle?*
- *What personal characteristics help one to survive in a situation like this? What kind of community supports are needed?*
- *Have you ever been in a really difficult situation? What did it take for you to survive?*
- *Knowing what we now know, how might we help refugees who have relocated in our community?*

Activity #2

STORY CLOTHS:
MIGRATION TALES FROM AROUND THE WORLD

Topic: Migration stories, including push-pull factors and resettlement

Age: 9 and up

Concepts:
- Differences and similarities in migration experiences
- Why people leave their homeland
- Human courage, determination, and resilience in the face of hardship

Strategies:
- Creating Art: Story Cloths
- Using Stories on the Same Theme
- Primary Sources: First Person Accounts
- Visual Tools: Mind Map and Chart

Resources:
- P. Deitz Shea, *The Whispering Cloth*
- Children's stories of family migrations
- Many sources of migration stories are referenced in the bibliography. You can also use interviews (students can interview people of older generations and then write the story in the first person), children's fiction and non-fiction

Activity Profile: This activity uses children's literature and first-person stories of migration as a basis for creating a piece of art to represent migration experiences. Students can do this activity with or without reading the specific literature selection *The Whispering Cloth*. After learning about the embroidered story cloths stitched in a refugee camp, students make a cloth for each family migration tale, using paint or crayon on paper or cloth.

Background: *The Whispering Cloth* tells the story of a young Hmong refugee from Laos, who lives in a Thai camp with her grandmother. Mai watches the women at the Widow's Store stitch pa'ndau (embroidered story cloths) to sell to traders. Taught to stitch by her grandmother, she hopes her pa'ndau will bring enough money to help them "fly from the camp" to join her cousins in America. However, a prized pa'ndau is only complete when it tells "your own story." Mai discovers her own story—her parents' death; her grandmother's escape with Mai on her back; the bullets and the boat crossing; the "soldiers in different clothes (who) took them to a crowded village inside a tall fence"; and finally, her dreams for the future. Her beautiful cloth, stitched in real life by You Yang who spent 17 years in Thai refugee camps, represents the lives of many refugees, many children's "hope in the midst of confinement and war."

STEPS:

Step 1. Begin by showing the class a picture of a pa'ndau (below) or bring in a story cloth from another country (story cloths are made in many parts of the world). Ask the students what they see in the cloth. If you have the book *The Whispering Cloth*, read and discuss the story. If not, tell students that pa'n-dau(s) are embroidered cloths that tell an important personal story. In refugee camps in Thailand, widows (and the young girls they taught) stitched pa'ndaus to sell to traders to earn money to survive and, for the lucky ones, to leave the camps. Tell students they are going to read stories of children from around the world who, like Mai, left their homes to move to another country. They are going to find out why these children left their homelands and how they survived and built new lives. Then the students will make pa'ndaus to tell the stories of these children.

Step 2. Divide the class in cooperative groups of approximately four students each. Give each group one migration story to read (three stories are provided here). Have the groups brainstorm the most important parts of the story on a mind map, such as the one below for Mai's story.

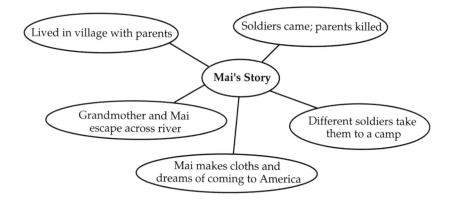

Bernard's Story

When I was a teenager, we lived in a village in Russia. Many Jewish people lived there. My father was a tailor. It was 1904. But the Czar didn't like Jews and one day there was a pogrom. Cossacks attacked the village, hurting many people and burning houses. When they left, we were angry. My friends and I wanted to protect the village so it would never happen again. We organized a group of young men to fight back. But the police found out about our organization and I was arrested. I spent many months in the Czar's prison and caught malaria. But then I managed to escape. I traveled by foot and cart and hopped trains when I could. I made my way from Russia across Europe working any job I could get along the way. Sometimes I was hungry and often tired. Finally, I was able to get on a boat for America.

The boat arrived at Ellis Island. There the immigration people changed my name because they couldn't pronounce Petroshenski. When I got to New York I took a job in a garment factory. I was nineteen when I arrived. At nineteen, I went to Kindergarten to learn English. The next year I went to college. (9)

Chol's Story

It was something like an accident when I ran away from my village. We were playing at about 5 o'clock when these people, the soldiers, came. We just ran. We didn't know where we were going to, we just ran…. I didn't see the soldiers, I just heard the shooting, the screaming and the bombing that went DUM, DUM, DUM, DUM…. It all just happened, like an accident, and we ran without anything—nothing—no food, no clothes, nothing.

In the day the sun is hot and your feet burn. So we walked at night when it is cold, because then you don't say all the time, 'I want water, I want water.'

Wild animals, lions, killed many people. But I was not scared because I was with many people, and when the lion came we would shout, 'Huh! Huh! Go! Go!' and then the lion would not kill us. So we just walked…. The big boys knew the way. I think God showed us the way….

On the roads you can't leave a person who just sits down. You must pinch him and say, 'Get up! Get up!' God has told you that you must take this person, he is life.

… After two months, we came to the Anyak tribe, who knew the way to Ethiopia. They helped us get fish and make dry fish. Not Bad! We would catch the fish standing in the river, but ten fish can't feed five million people, and everybody wanted some. So, we would catch and give to the next person. We stood in a line in the river….

To go to Ethiopia, to the Panyido refugee camp, there was a big river we had to swim across…. Some people who did not know how to swim refused to go…. When you have two or three brothers they can help. We try this way, that way, every way. There were strings and ropes to help pull people across. Many people stayed to teach themselves how to swim….

Now I live with other boys in Kakuma (in a refugee camp in Kenya). We cook for ourselves and build our own homes. I like playing basketball, but there is also football and school if you would like.

We are town people now, we have shoes and a shirt, you see? I say, let us stay here where it is safe….Now we want to learn. One day I will be an engineer to build Sudan like the other countries in Africa.[10]

Wilfredo's Story

When I was little, we lived in San Ramon, El Salvador. In the whole pueblito there were only five houses. It had more trees than houses!

My best friend was Victor. We played marbles in the road near my house. When we got tired of that, we cut carao. We cracked it open and made a drink with the honey seeds. It is called fresco de carao. Es sabroso!

When I was six, Victor moved to the United States with his family. The United States was so far away that I knew I would never see him again. Then Mama went there too. I didn't want her to leave, but she was worried that my grandmother would be left alone with only a little money. Mama hoped she could make more money in the United States.

I went to live with my grandmother. I call her abuelita. She lived in the city of San Salvador, the capital of El Salvador. Even though it was a big city, there were trees and fields and mountains close by. Sometimes I got up early to go hiking with my companeros. I love the fields and hills and rivers of my country.

One day I got a letter from Mama. She wrote that she was coming to El Salvador for a visit, and then she would bring me back to the United States with her.

I didn't want to leave abuelita, my companeros and the mountains. I was afraid I would be lonely. But I wanted to be with Mama again. Mama said I wouldn't be lonely in the United States because my aunt, my uncle and my cousins lived there.

We came to San Francisco right before school started. On the first day of school, I met Jose. He is Mexicano. He introduced me to my teacher and some of the other kids in the class....We talked in Spanish. I was so glad he was there!

One day a new boy came to our class. I said hello to him. He looked at me for a long time. Then he said, "I think I know you.... I remember now. You were my friend in San Ramon. Do you remember me?"

I looked at him and then we laughed. It was Victor! We shook hands. I was so happy to see my oldest friend from El Salvador in my new country![11]

Step 3. After mind-mapping the parts of the story, students next add feelings they think the family had at various points in their journey and personal strengths of the people that helped them survive (courage, for example).

Step 4. After the group has decided on the most meaningful parts of the story, they begin making the pa'ndau. Students paint or draw a decorative border around the edges of a large sheet or cloth (alternatively, you can use felt cloth with cut-out felt story pieces pasted on). Divide the large sheet in sections, representing parts of the story. Referring to their mind maps, have students map out the story on smaller squares. Each student in the group will be responsible for making one part of the story on the smaller square to complete the larger pa'ndau for the group. Ask students to discuss how the people would feel in each story square and how they might show those feelings in the drawings (with color, with gesture, with facial expressions). The last square should represent a hope for the future (like Mai's in *The Whispering Cloth*). To enrich the imagination, you might bring books with pictures of the countryside where the stories take place. The groups may look at them as they draw.

At the end of *The Whispering Cloth*, Mai must decide how much her cloth is worth. Should she sell it to the traders, perhaps earning enough money to leave the camp? She decides that it is priceless, and that she will not sell it. At the end of this activity, each student group should decide whether or not to sell their cloth and why? What is its value?

Step 5. Each group presents its pa'ndau and tells the story. Or, they hold up the pa'ndau and ask the other students what they think it represents. Discuss how the pa'ndaus are similar? different? Make a chart of differences and similarities:

	Mai's story	Bernard's story	Wilfredo's story	Chol's story
Reasons for leaving				
Reasons to come to new country				
Difficulties				
Joys and hopes				

In closing, discuss:

– *What have we learned about why people move?*
– *What choices have people had to make in migrating?*
– *How does this relate to our own lives?*

Activity #3
THE TRAIL OF TEARS

Topic:	The forced removal of the indigenous people from their ancestral homelands
Age:	8–12
Concepts:	• Forced migration • Multiple perspectives on one event
Strategies:	• Primary Sources: Memoirs, Letters, Documents • Visual Tools: Charting Multiple Perspectives on One Event • Writing Sentence Stems • "What if…?" Writing • A Pattern of Questions
Resources:	• Trail of Tears Information and Quotation Sheet (included on **page 90–92**) • Suggested secondary sources: D. Fremon, *The Trail of Tears*; N. Claire, *The Cherokee Indians*; Children's literature: D. & T. Hoobler, *The Trail on Which They Wept*; Painting by Robert Lindneux, *"The Trail of Tears"* (this painting is widely reprinted in books about the Cherokee removal) • You can adapt questions from the "Talking Photos" strategy in "Children at Work"

Activity Profile: Students use primary sources to identify multiple perspectives in a major conflict in history. This format can be used to study any major conflict in history. This particular activity is about the removal of the Cherokee from the southeastern United States in the 1830s. Students chart the different perspectives of the Cherokees, white settlers, soldiers and government officials. They develop their understanding of these points of view by writing in the voice of particular historical groups. Then, given those perspectives, they imagine an alternative solution to the problem, and write how history could have been different.

Historical Background: In the 1830s, after a series of treaties in which Cherokee land was exchanged for peace with the settlers in the southeastern United States, the Cherokee were forced to leave their ancestral homeland. This happened in spite of a United States Supreme Court decision making such an order illegal and unconstitutional. This order was carried out by the United States Army. Thousands of Cherokee were forcibly removed from their homes and taken to stockades, later to be forced to walk hundreds of miles to reservations west of the Mississippi River. The perspectives of those involved (white settlers, U.S. soldiers, Cherokees differed dramatically. Within the Cherokee Nation, too, there was more than one view of what to do. This activity can be part of a larger study in which students consult other sources for background information leading up to the forced march called the "Trail of Tears."

STEPS

Step 1. Read the quotations below. (Alternatively, place in overhead projector, or hand out a printed page for students to read.)

. . . .

We the great mass of the people think only of the love we have of our land…we do love the land where we were brought up. We will never let our hold to this land go…to let it go it will be like throwing away…[our] mother that gave…[us] birth.

— Cherokee Indians,
letter from tribal members to John Ross, principal chief[12]

I saw the helpless Cherokee arrested and dragged from their homes, and driven at the bayonet point into the stockades. And in the chill of a drizzling rain on an October morning I saw them loaded like cattle or sheep into six hundred and forty-five wagons and started toward the west.

One can never forget the sadness and solemnity of that morning. Chief John Ross led in prayer and when the bugle sounded and the wagons started rolling many of the children rose to their feet and waved their little hands good-bye to their mountain homes, knowing they were leaving them forever.

— John Burnett, United States soldier [13]

When the soldiers came to my house, my father wanted to fight, but my mother told him that the soldiers would kill him if he did. They drove us out of our house..... After they took us away, my mother begged them to let her go back and get some bedding. So they let her go back and she brought what bedding and a few cooking utensils she could carry and we left behind all our other household possessions.

— Rebecca Neugin, Cherokee child[14]

. . . .

Step 2. Prompt your students' thinking about these statements by asking questions that begin with their ideas and their background knowledge. For example:

– *Who do you think is speaking these words?*
– *Have you ever felt as strongly about something as the person who wrote the first statement?*
– *What could have happened between the time the first statement was made and the time the second was made?*

Continue with questions such as the ones below that review the historical context. Here, some gaps in students' knowledge may appear. Note gaps and go on to Step 3.

– *What was going on in the United States at this time?*
– *What might you already know about the Cherokee and the white settlers?*
– *Why were the Cherokee "driven at the bayonet point into the stockades?"*

Step 3. Have students gather information that will help them identify different perspectives on the United States government's decision to remove the Cherokee from Georgia. In addition to the Quotation and Perspectives Information Sheets provided here, your resources could include library books, maps, photographs, facsimiles, and realia. After students have had a chance to read and learn more about the historical background and events leading to the removal, gather class together to develop profiles of the different perspectives.

THE TRAIL OF TEARS
PERSPECTIVES INFORMATION SHEET

Cherokee Perspectives

1. The last memorial the Cherokee sent to the United States stated:

   The title of the Cherokee people to their lands is the most ancient, pure and absolute known to man; its date is beyond human record... and cannot... be dissolved by the expulsion of the Nation from its own territory.
   — Cherokee Tribal Members,
   letter to United States government[15]

2. The majority of the Cherokee called their Chief, John Ross a hero for standing up to United States President, Andrew Jackson. Under his leadership, the Cherokee resisted removal for as long as they could, and went about their life "as usual."

   The Cherokee are not foreigners, but the original inhabitants of America...they now stand on the soil of their own territory, and they cannot recognize the sovereignty of any state within the limits of their territory." — John Ross[16]

3. John Ridge was a Cherokee leader who recommended that they move west peacefully. He convinced senators who had once supported the Cherokee cause to write a removal treaty, which gave $4.5 million to the Cherokee. Without the authority of the Cherokee Nation, Ridge signed this treaty. When he brought it back to the Nation for approval, he was treated as an outcast by most of his people. He and a group of his supporters went west, thinking this was the best decision.

4. The soldiers came and forced the people into the stockades. Finally, after John Ross saw that all was lost, he organized the march to the Western territory. This march later became known as "The Trail of Tears."

Settler Perspectives

1. White settlers, builders, plantation owners who thirsted for more land and resources for their plantations, and businesses were among those who pressured the government to remove the Cherokee. That these lands had been occupied by people for centuries mattered not to the newcomers. What did matter were the opportunities for more land, resources, workers, wealth and comfort.

2. In 1830, gold was discovered in the Georgia Cherokee Hills. This brought even more white settlers into the Cherokee Nation.

3. Davy Crockett, the famous frontiersman who was a congressional representative from Tennessee, said of the Indian Removal Act:

   I believed it was a wicked, unjust measure, ...I voted against this Indian bill, and my conscience yet tells me that I gave a good honest vote.

   — Davy Crockett[17]

Soldier Perspectives

1. In 1838, newly elected President Van Buren ordered General Winfield Scott to "get the Indians out of Georgia, sir!" The General advised the Cherokee to leave their homes peacefully, trying to prevent an outbreak of violence between the soldiers and the Indians.[18]

2. A Georgian who volunteered as a soldier in the removal later said:

   I saw the Civil War and have seen men shot to pieces and slaughtered by the thousands, but the Cherokee removal was the cruelest work I ever saw. — a Georgian Volunteer[19]

Government Perspectives

1. In 1791, Thomas Jefferson was Secretary of State. He said, "*I am of the opinion. . . that the Indians have a right to the occupation of their lands, independent of the state within those chartered limits they happen to be: That until they cede them by treaty, no act of the state can give them right to such lands.*" Later, when he became President, he encouraged the Cherokee to move west into the territory known as the Louisiana Purchase. When some of the Cherokee followed his advice and moved to Arkansas, they pushed other Indians, the Osage, off of their land.[20]

2. When Andrew Jackson ran for president in 1828, one of his campaign promises was to remove the Cherokee from the state of Georgia. As President, he claimed that he couldn't protect the Cherokee from being harassed by the Georgian plantation owners and they would be safer if they moved. He brought the Indian Removal Act before the Congress. The Removal Bill said that the United States government could remove Indians from the homes and land, and send them to live west of the Mississippi.

3. In 1827, the Georgia State Legislature declared that, *"all the lands, appropriated, and unappropriated which lie within the conventional limits of Georgia belong to her absolutely...the Indians are tenants at her will."*   — Georgia State Legislature[21]

4. In 1832, the United States Supreme Court decided that the Cherokee Nation was a sovereign nation, entitled to their land. Chief Justice Marshall wrote, *"The acts of Georgia are repugnant to the Constitution, laws and treaties of the United States."* In the meantime, the Governor of Georgia had declared that *"the State of Georgia is not accountable to the Supreme Court,"* and President Jackson openly refused to protect the Indians.
    — Chief Justice Marshall[22]

Step 4. Chart the different perspectives using a visual organizer. List the groups on the left as below, and ask students to think through what would be the corresponding positions, on the right. Ask students to find different Cherokee positions and various government positions. Ask students who might have voted for the government officials representing different positions. The chart might look like this:

GROUP	POSITION
The Cherokee	Wanted to work out a compromise...*(to continue living and working on ancestral lands, continue to take on ways of the white community while retaining some Cherokee values and customs, and to contribute to the larger United States through agriculture and business).* Wanted to...*(sell land to whites and move west).* Wanted to...*(stay and fight).*
The white settlers	Wanted to...*(build their own farms and businesses on Cherokee land. Willing to defy Federal law and Supreme Court ruling to get what they wanted).*
Government officials and others supporting Removal	Thought that...*(the settlers should be able to move onto Indian land. Indians should move west).*

Government officials and others opposing Removal	Thought that...(*the settlers and government should respect the rights of Cherokee to live on their own land*).
United States soldiers who participated in the Removal	Thought that...(*they had to follow orders from President van Buren and General Scott. Tried to be kind to the Cherokee while taking them from their homes, imprisoning them in stockades, forcing their trek to reservation in Oklahoma.*)

Step 5. Writing Sentence Stems from Different Perspectives. Students take on the viewpoint of either the Cherokee, settlers or government officials. Using the chart and other information, each group or pair completes a set of sentence stems to "voice" the position of one of these groups in the 1830s.
Sample sentence stems:
   "We want... ."
   "We believe... ."
   "We don't understand... ."
   "We need... ."
   "We feel... . "

Step 6. "What If...? " Writing. Ask students to imagine themselves back in the 1830s. Could they have made a better decision than the one which resulted in the Trail of Tears? What if history had taken a different course? Brainstorm alternative solutions to the conflict between the Cherokee and the white settlers. List the pros and cons of each solution. Students will write "What if...?" stories in the first person, telling about what would have happened if they had solved the problem in another way.

After students have shared their "What if...?" solutions, conclude by discussing the following question:

– *How does this event in history affect our lives today?*

Activity #4

RADIO MESSAGE CENTER:
VOICES OF THE CHILDREN OF FARMWORKERS

Topic: Migrant labor

Age: 8–12

Concepts:
- Internal migration
- Relocating for work and moving frequently
- Keeping communities together despite relocation
- People who supply our foods

Strategies:
- Combining Children's Literature with Primary Sources
- First Person Writing: Radio Messages
- Visual Tool: Charting
- A Pattern of Questions

Resources:
- Sample Radio Message (included)
- Arthur Dorros, *Radio Man*
- Bibliography of children's books on migrant labor
- Jose's story (included)

Historical Summary: Migrant workers play an important role in economies all over the world. In Europe, migrant workers come from Italy, Spain, Greece, Turkey, Yugoslavia and North Africa. Some workers return to their home countries when work contracts are completed; some remain. Historically, immigration policy debates and feelings about foreign workers have followed the ebbs and flows of the economy. When there is a labor shortage, migrant workers have been lured across borders to fill the need for low-wage work. Periods of recession are often accompanied by backlashes against foreign workers perceived to be taking jobs away from native workers. In the United States, Mexican and Mexican-American farmworkers have harvested broccoli, lettuce, strawberries, grapes and other crops. They work long hours, often seven days a week, in back-breaking work, planting, picking and packing fruits and vegetables for minimal wages. Sometimes their wages are insufficient to feed and house their families. Farmworker families move frequently to find work. Their children sometimes help in the fields and change schools frequently.

Activity Profile: In this activity, students write and perform radio messages to send to friends left behind when migrant farmworker families move to follow the harvests. After reading the fictional picture book *Radio Man,* they thoughtfully inquire about similarities and differences between their own lives and those of farmworker children. The radio messages they write are based on the lives of real children they read about in brief autobiographies (included on **page 95–98**). Writing personal messages to friends they miss puts students in an empathic stance, as they try to imagine what it might be like without their own best friend to talk to about the feelings and events of their daily lives. Finally, students integrate what they have learned and what they feel about it by performing their messages which powerfully convey a child's view of the migrant experience.

This activity sequence may be done with or without the book *Radio Man,* or by substituting literature about migrant workers in your own context (omit Step 3 and adapt Step 4).

Book Summary: *Radio Man* is the story of a farmworker family, traveling most of each year to find work picking fruits and vegetables. As they follow the harvest, the familiar voices of the Spanish radio stations are companions, helping them keep track of friends and relatives left behind. For Diego, the book's young protagonist, the radio messages are deeply personal. He misses his friend David and contacts him by sending his own radio message.

STEPS:

Preparation. Ask one of your students to help you make a radio message on audiotape. The student can record or read Manuel's Radio Message provided below.

Manuel's Radio Message

Ola! This is Manuel in Castroville, California, United States. I would like to send a message to Benja, my best friend. He used to live next door. But his family had to move. They are probably working in other fields picking fruit—but I'm not sure where they live now.

Benja, I miss you! If you were here, we could play outside after school on the days I don't have to help my parents pick strawberries, lettuce and flowers. I still like my school here, but it is not the

---

same without you. We get breakfast and lunch there. I wish I could send you the book about camiones (trucks) I got from the free book program! I loved it and I am making my own book about trailers, and one about a rabbit who gets chased out of his hole and moves to a big safe house underground made of mud.

Where do you live now, Benja? Have you made new friends? I hope you live in a bigger house.

Adios, Benja. I hope you hear me. If you do, send me a message on the radio so I know where you are.

— *Manuel*

Step 1. Play the radio announcement or have student read it aloud. If you have a bilingual class, play the announcement in both languages.

Step 2. Ask questions to help students make a personal connection to what they are hearing.

– *What do you hear? Who is talking? To whom is she or he talking?*
– *Why are they using the radio?*
– *How do you talk to your friends or relatives? How do you send messages?*
– *What if there was no phone number or mailing address?*
– *Have you ever heard similar announcements on the radio?*

Step 3. Read *Radio Man* (or other literature about migrant workers within your own country). As you read, students dialogue with the text and illustrations. For example, ask students what they observe in the pictures and text about Diego's day, his room, his morning, etc. Younger students can draw a picture of their morning and compare to Diego's.

Step 4. Chart similarities and differences between Diego's life and the lives of your students. Make the chart on an overhead projector or chalkboard. Model how to fill it in by asking students what they might say about their own family, work, school, etc. Write information in the appropriate squares. Then begin to record ideas about Diego's life, using evidence from the book. As you model, each child should make her own individual chart. (Note: Information for Jose and Manuel are not to be filled in until Step 5.)

	work	family	school	friends	communi- cation with family and friends
me					
Diego					
Jose					
Manuel					

Step 5. Once students have thought about Diego's daily life in relation to their own, they begin to read about other migrant worker children. You may choose to use Jose's story (below), or Manuel's Radio Message (included before Step 1), other fiction, or non-fiction books about migrant workers. As students read, they continue to fill in the comparison chart for other farmworkers.

José's Story

José is nine years old. He lives with his mother, father, brothers, sisters, cousins and aunts and uncles. All the older people in his whole family work in the fields, including his older brothers and cousins. His grandparents live in Mexico now. They used to work in the fields, too. He doesn't get to see them, and he doesn't know them.

José is in his third year of school. He likes going to school "to learn because then you know things." He is learning to speak English, but he likes to speak Spanish because then people understand him better. He is learning to read and write. He likes learning about people like the Native Americans and the Mayans. He is proud of his drawing and writing. Once in a while, when he is at school, José gets headaches and has to go to the nurse's office.

Sometimes, instead of going to school, José goes with his father out to the strawberry fields to help out. He enjoys watching the birds and sometimes he gets to eat strawberries. But on the way home when it is muddy and dark, he gets tired and cold. When he helps in the fields, he finds it difficult to do his homework, and he is tired in school the next day. "It is hard to work and go to school at the same time," he says. Sometimes his aunts and cousins are there in the fields, too. He can play games like tag in the fields. At home, he plays with his sisters and his cousins. He helps watch the younger children play in the driveway.

José goes back and forth between wanting to work in the fields when he gets older and wanting to stay in school. One time he will say, "I like coming to school better than I like working in the fields…. The people who haven't gone to school, they work in the fields." Another time he will say, "When I'm bigger, I want to be a field worker and work in the strawberries because I like to work…."

— Adapted from *Voices from the Fields: Children of Migrant Farmworkers Tell Their Stories*, by S. Beth Atkin

Step 6. As the charts will show, moving often means a lot of good-byes. Friends and relatives are missed. Sometimes it's hard to locate them and keep in touch. Spanish call-in stations, like the Voz de La Frontera in the story provide one way to get messages to loved ones. In this final activity, students use the information they've learned about real farmworker children to write a message they will send to a friend.

Ask students to choose a child they have read about. Instruct them to take the role of one of the children and write a radio message to a friend. Encourage students to use the information in the chart to inform their writing. They are writing in the voice of the child (first person).

Step 7. Have students perform and record (if possible) their radio messages. See **page 13** in Chapter 2 for an example of a radio message written by Michael, age 10, after reading portions of S. Beth Atkin's *Voices from the Field*.

SNAPSHOTS OF LIFE IN MY NEW COUNTRY

Topic:	Problems faced by recent immigrants
Age:	8 and up
Concepts:	• Community-building • Inclusion • Civic action
Strategies:	• Problem–Solving Vignettes • Visual Tools: Venn Diagrams; Mind Maps • Primary Sources and Fiction • "What If… ?" Writing
Resources:	• Shiromani's Story (included) • Set of vignettes written on Snapshot Cards (included) • Vignettes #1 & 3 are excerpted from *Got Me A Story To Tell*, by S. Yee and L. Kokin, Vignette #4 is excerpted from *Who Belongs Here?* by M.B. Knight. Other good sources of vignettes might include students' own stories and fictional accounts of immigration experiences (see bibliography)

Activity Profile: Students are given problem cards describing situations and impressions of children who have recently immigrated to a new country. These cards are called Snapshot Cards. First with the whole group, and then in small groups, students identify the problems and feelings of the newcomer on a card. Then, using Venn Diagrams, students compare situations they themselves have faced to problems the newcomer is facing. Finally, they create "What If…?" sheets, diagramming things individuals, schools, neighborhoods or government could do to help newcomers feel more welcome.

STEPS

Step 1. Distribute copies of Shiromani's story (on page 100) to students. Ask them to follow along as you read it aloud.

Shiromani's Story

I am Hindu. My great-grandparents came to Fiji from India a long time ago. I am ten years old. I can speak two languages. I like to speak English with my friends at school and Hindi at home.

I went to school, but nobody talked to me there. A boy said, "You are stupid. You don't know English. I don't like you." I didn't say anything to him. I wanted to say, "When you came to this world you didn't speak English either."

I was lonely in [my new country.] Even the Hindu people [here] were different. Some of them don't want to talk Hindi, only English. That means they want to forget where they're from. I want to be my own, too. I like to be Fiji.

— from *Got Me A Story To Tell*, by Yee and Kokin

Step 2. Ask students:

- What did you hear Shiromani saying?
- What do you think Shiromani is feeling? As students respond, record words on the board.

anger   sadness   confusion

Step 3. Ask what problems Shiromani tells us about. Do a "whip around" to identify as many issues contained in the vignette as possible. Ask the first student to name a problem. Each successive student in turn names another problem or adds to the response as you "whip around" the classroom. Mind-map the students' ideas on the chalkboard.

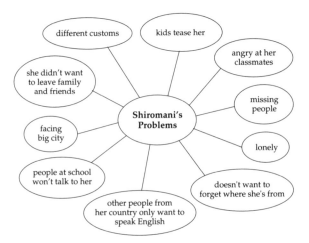

Ask students if they've ever experienced any of these problems? Generate one or two examples.

Step 4. Pair each student with another. In partners, students make a Venn Diagram comparing problems they have faced to problems Shiromani is facing. Afterwards, have volunteers report out to the larger group.

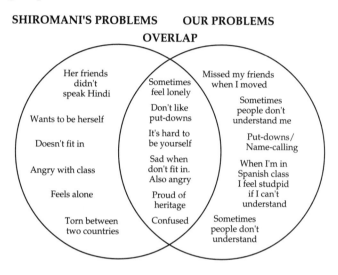

SHIROMANI'S PROBLEMS   OUR PROBLEMS

OVERLAP

Her friends didn't speak Hindi

Wants to be herself

Doesn't fit in

Angry with class

Feels alone

Torn between two countries

Sometimes feel lonely

Don't like put-downs

It's hard to be yourself

Sad when don't fit in. Also angry

Proud of heritage

Confused

Missed my friends when I moved

Sometimes people don't understand me

Put-downs/ Name-calling

When I'm in Spanish class I feel studpid if I can't understand

Sometimes people don't understand

Step 5. Ask each pair of students to join a second pair. Give each group of four one of the **Snapshot Cards**. Each card contains a scenario written by a child who is a recent immigrant.

SNAPSHOT CARDS

The group reads the card and answers these two questions together:

– *Does the person who wrote your card notice anything about this country that you hadn't thought about before? What can you learn from him or her?*
– *What problems is the person in the vignette having?*

Snapshot Card #1

When we first came to [my new country] , I didn't have so much fun. No one played with me….Some of them said that I was stupid because I couldn't speak English like them. They yelled, "Chinese girl! Chinese girl!" And then they ran away from me. So just Ed and I played together. Or I played by myself. Once near my apartment, two girls hid from me. Then when I walked near them, they came out and pulled my hair. They pulled it so hard that I cried. I don't know why they wanted to hurt me like that. After that Mommy didn't want me to play outside anymore….I wished I was back in Hong Kong….[There] they were kind to me.

Snapshot Card #2

On my first day of school, I was scared to go out in the yard at lunch time. Everyone was screaming. What were they saying? All the kids had friends and were playing games that I didn't know how to play. There were balls flying everywhere. I couldn't find the teacher. I was afraid I would be left out. Someone threw a ball to me, but I didn't know where to throw it. Then Johanna came and smiled and showed me what to do.

Snapshot Card #3

Some kids were nice to me at school, like Vivian and Shabnam. When we eat lunch in school and they have beef, I won't eat it. In the Hindu religion, cows are special animals, so you can't eat their meat. When Vivian sees that I don't eat, then she doesn't eat either. I say, "How come you don't eat it?" She says, "I don't like when you don't eat it."

Snapshot Card #4

Nary was upset that his classmates didn't understand how it felt to be a refugee. He told his teacher and together they planned a lesson for his social studies class. Each student pretended to be a refugee. The students had to try to convince non-English-speaking guards that they were refugees seeking asylum. Patting his stomach, one student said,"thuc an," the Vietnamese word for food. Another student said "dom"as she built the shape of a house with her fingers; her grandmother had taught her the Polish word for home. The lesson reminded Nary of his own experiences and he told his classmates that no one should have to be a refugee. He wished that everyone would have enough food and that all the guns would be taken away.

Step 6. Now each group makes a "What if...?" mind map on a large sheet of paper. What if things were different for the person who wrote your card? Brainstorm some ideas to help make things better for someone like the person on your card, perhaps a new student at your school or in your neighborhood. Use your imagination. What could *you* do? What could *someone else* do? Think of things you could do as individuals, things the school could do, things the neighbors or government could do. Write your group's ideas on the "What If...?" mind map.

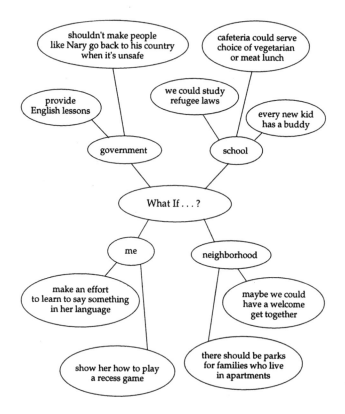

Step 7. Post all the "What if...?" sheets at the front of the classroom. Discuss them as a whole class.

OPTIONAL: TAKING ACTION

Option 1. After the sheets are posted, vote on the best ideas in each category. What is the best idea of something we can do as individuals? as a school? as a community? What would we like the government to do? Choosing one idea, have the class make an action plan outlining steps to take. Neighborhood issues or laws can be researched. Who decides on policies? How are community policies changed? The class might write letters to the appropriate authorities, or write editorials for a local paper, etc. One class of seven-year-olds in Chicago, USA managed to get a street renamed when students argued through local government that there were no streets named for African-American women.

Option 2. Tell students: Imagine for the day that your family has just moved to this city and this is your first day at school. Take a clipboard and pencil. As you go through your normal day in school, walk around the school with a newcomer's eyes. Jot down impressions. What seems strange or curious to you? What is unwelcoming or scary? What would make things better for you as a newcomer?

The next day, pool the information on a chart at the front of the class and discuss. Ask students to pretend now that they have been elected to the school's Student Council or School Welcoming Committee. Vote on two important things the Student Council and Welcoming Committee could change at the school to create a welcoming environment for new students.

CHAPTER SEVEN

THROUGH CONFLICT

AND CHANGE

Perspective-taking activities

Jesse Reiter-Skolnick

Introduction

Conflict is a part of our everyday life. On the play-
ground, observe students disputing the rules of a game, arguing

over who pushed whom, or whose turn it is to get the new ball at recess. At home, siblings may fight, parents may describe a battle at work and neighbors may bicker over unkempt yards, unleashed dogs and late-night parties.

In addition to these interpersonal disputes, conflict is inherent in societies, especially where inequalities exist. Social and economic differences set up a potential for conflict and a pressure for change.

As Gail Sadalla, Meg Holmberg and Jim Halligan explain in *Conflict Resolution: An Elementary Curriculum*, "conflict is often rooted in differences between people—differences in their ways of perceiving the world, their assumptions about other people, the values by which they live their lives, and the ways in which they express themselves."[23]

If conflict is about difference, then understanding conflict and resolving conflict (change) has to involve learning about perspectives. Indeed, at points of conflict, differences in perspectives that underlie our "normal" lives are most clearly and powerfully revealed. We might not even realize that these differences exist, as we take for granted that other people see the world as we do, and want the same kinds of change.

Because conflicts often expose different views, they can provide opportunities for perspective-taking. Interpersonally, "when a conflict motivates us to take the time to explore and understand [our] differences, we can learn about ourselves and others... [and it] may help us build stronger, deeper relationships...."[24] Similarly, studying social conflicts in history or current events provides students with opportunities to see why different groups of people, with various positions in society fight and what these people want to change.

For example, many historical conflicts have centered around "development" and "expansion." How might development look from the perspective of residents in surrounding communities? To companies? To workers? To women or men? To indigenous peoples of the rain forests? To consumers of rain forest products? What did westward expansion in North America look like to Plains Indians who saw the wagon trains going through? To "land-poor" families in the east? To African-Americans? To mining companies? To workers and homesteaders already out west? In these different views, where lies the potential for conflict?

When we were in school, we got the impression that everyone who fought on the same side of a battle wanted the same thing.

Our texts often described conflicts from the perspective of the victors or dominant group, interpreting the meaning of the struggle and its outcome accordingly. For example, we were told that American colonists fought for "freedom" in the American Revolution, and that it resulted in "independence." We never examined the word "freedom" from different perspectives. What kinds of freedoms (economic, political, legal) motivated different men and women to fight and risk their lives? Did they all see freedom in the same way? A 10-year-old asked this question and came up with the following answer.

> Freedom did not mean the same thing to all groups in American society during the Revolutionary period. Freedom for Blacks did not mean the same as freedom for rich white merchants. Blacks were slaves. They wanted to be set free. Freedom for merchants was freedom from taxes. Native Americans had freedom before the white men came—to live and roam where they wanted. That's the kind of freedom they wanted. Women were freer than Blacks and Indians, but not free as white men. Women could not vote, own land or own a business. Freedom meant being able to do these things. Did all these people fight for the same thing? When the revolution was over, did they get what they wanted or fought for? Then what happened?

This child is learning to unravel what he reads in history books by asking questions about a conflict from multiple perspectives. We'd like to teach our students to become critical historians, learning to look for the diverse groups who participated in struggles for change and inquiring about them. We want our students to ask questions such as: How can I find out who was there and what they really wanted or what they were fighting for? Did they get what they wanted (or part of it) when the conflict was over? If not, how does that affect the battles yet to be fought? In this chapter, we present activities that investigate periods of turbulence, change and incidents of civic disturbance. The methods we use help students to view conflicts from multiple perspectives, break them apart, learn to identify and give voice to key groups reacting to events and taking actions for change.

One critical event in a period of turmoil or rapid change can tell us a lot about people's experiences over time. Whether you study a historical or a contemporary incident, you as a teacher can use such critical incidents as a concrete way of investigating broader issues. These incidents help students see that different people can be part of the same event and view it differently, depending on their past and present experiences.

Two activities in this chapter focus on historical instances of conflict: the forced internment of Japanese-Americans and Japanese-Canadians during World War II ("No Loyal Citizen"); and Revolution as seen through the eyes of men and women of different ethnic and economic groups ("People in the Revolution"). These activities use children's literature, jigsaw dialogue and simulation to enable students to take another's perspective in a conflict.

Three other activities illustrate how to use current conflicts to study social issues from multiple perspectives. When there is a crisis that deeply affects a community, activities can help students express their views, understand other views and constructively consider next steps. In "The Spirits at Castlelake Beach" and "Owls and Jobs," art is the vehicle for exploring feelings of diverse groups about land use, economic development and the preservation of culturally special places and natural habitats. "Newcomers in Our Town" uses the dialogue poem to help students juxtapose two views of recent immigration into a community. Students learn the skills of identifying different viewpoints, voicing views, and listening to various groups in these social conflicts. It is our hope that they will begin to see the applicability of such skills in daily personal conflicts as well. School conflict resolution programs foster the development of similar skills.

Activity #1
"NO LOYAL CITIZEN..."

Topic:	Japanese-American and Japanese-Canadian internment during World War II.
Age:	8 and up
Concepts:	• Rights and responsibilities in a democratic society • Forced migration • Racism
Strategies:	• Writing Dialogue • Children's Literature: Focusing on Critical Decision-Making Moments • Dramatic Arts: Performing Dialogue

Resources:
- Children's historical fiction: Y. Uchida, *Journey To Topaz,*
- Optional: historical photographs or artwork from the internment camps: L.D. Brimner, *Voices From the Camps*

Historical Background: Not all people who migrate do so voluntarily in order to seek a better life. Historically, many peoples have been forced to leave their homes under threat of death or incarceration, because of incursions on their land, unjust government policies, or the impact of war. Examples are the removal of Native Americans from their homelands to reservations, the removal of Africans to the United States, the Nazi relocation of Jews to concentration camps during World War II, and the relocation and internment of Japanese-Americans and Japanese-Canadians during World War II.

Few of us realize that people living next door to us may once have been told to pack up their belongings, with only a few hours notice, and move to an internment camp. We want our students to think about what it might mean to lose their home, family business, liberty and rights. What might it feel like? How and why did such things happen and how can we prevent them from happening again? What is the impact of these events on peoples' lives through successive generations?

Activity Profile: This activity uses a dramatic decision-making moment in historical fiction to help students understand what it was like for a Japanese-Canadian or Japanese-American family to move to an internment camp during World War II. The activity sequence may be used with other children's literature to investigate multiple perspectives on any historical event of significance in your curriculum. Choose a critical decision-making moment in the book. Read a passage from the book describing this dramatic moment to the class. To create the jigsaw dialogue, divide students into *expert groups* of approximately five students each. Each group is assigned to become the expert on one character in the book. Guided by a set of questions, each "expert" group thinks through their character's reactions, feelings and thoughts about the event in the story. Students search the book for evidence. They then write their character's response or decision. Students are then re-divided into *family groups* that include one student from every expert group. In the family group, each expert presents her character's response, creating a character dialogue that can be performed as readers' theater.

Story Summary: *Journey to Topaz* views the events of World War II through the eyes of eleven-year-old Yuki, a Japanese-American girl whose family was moved to a dismal desert internment camp called Topaz. In Chapter 16 of the book, the army recruiters come to the camp and ask Yuki's older brother, Ken, to serve in the army and fight the Japanese. Through this cooperative learning jigsaw activity, students wrestle with the concept of rights and responsibilities by taking the perspectives of five different characters in the novel. The five characters are: Yuki and Ken, their mother and father, and Mr.Toda, their neighbor. The characters must help Ken decide whether to serve in the United States Army despite the denial of rights to his family.

STEPS

(Preparation) Before beginning the jigsaw activity, you may choose to help students connect personally to the topic by doing one of the following:

> – Ask students to think about a time when they felt they were denied their rights unfairly. Did they ever feel they had responsibilities, but no rights? What might that mean?

OR

> – Show posters or photos from the camps, asking students what they observe and what their reactions might be if they were someone in the photo.

Step 1. Read an excerpt from the book, at a moment of decision-making. In this example, read the following excerpt from Chapter 16 in *Journey to Topaz.*

> *It was in the cold bleakness of February that the army recruiters from the War Department arrived in Topaz.*
> *"I wonder why they've come now?" Mother asked.*
> *"I thought the army wasn't accepting Nisei because of their ancestry."*
> *"That's right, they weren't," Ken explained. "But now the Secretary of War says they want to form a special all-Nisei combat team."*
> *"Why?" Yuki wondered. "Why can't they just join up like everybody else?"*
> *The army recruiter who stood in front of the group was handsome in his neatly pressed uniform and his sun-bleached hair. He told them how the President felt that all loyal Americans regardless of race should be permitted to exercise their responsibilities as citizens.*

Step 2. Ask the following critical-thinking questions:

– *What are the responsibilities the army recruiter is talking about?*
– *Do you think it is fair of him to ask this of the Nisei?*
– *How would you respond if you were in the shoes of people at the camp?*

Step 3. Assign students to like-character "expert" groups. In these groups, four to five students discuss one character's perspective. The following instruction sheet is given to all groups.

Group Instruction Sheet
In 1943, President Roosevelt declared that "no loyal citizen," regardless of ancestry, should be denied the democratic right to exercise the responsibilities of a citizen to serve in the army.

In your groups, discuss how your character would respond to what the army recruiter said in the above quote from *Journey to Topaz*. Write down at least three things he or she would say. Later, each of you will represent your character in a family group meeting, when all the characters will have a dialogue.

The following questions will help you start your group discussion:

1. What rights does your character have?
2. What rights has she or he been denied?
3. What are your character's responsibilities?
4. Did your character fulfill or ignore his responsibilities?
5. What do you think are the governments' responsibilities toward your character?
6. Look in the book for things your character says or does to support your answer.

Step 4. From the expert groups in Step 3, create new family groups that include one character from every group above. These new family groups each have one student expert representing Yuki, Ken, Mom, Dad and Mr. Toda.

Instruct the new group to create a dialogue in which each character gives advice to Ken to help him decide whether to serve in the army despite the fact that his family has been denied its civic rights in the camp.

Step 5 (optional). Create a performance from the dialogues. Have each family group practice a dramatic presentation of the different characters' views by going around the circle as each character stands and reads his or her advice to Ken. Each group then presents to the class. You may want to suggest a repeating line to create a voice for each character. For example,

"I am the voice of Yuki, Ken's sister"
"I am the voice of Ken, the one asked to serve"
"I am the mother of the one asked to fight"

Activity #2
PEOPLE IN THE REVOLUTION:
HISTORIAN'S SIMULATION WORKSHOP

Topic: Any revolution, colonial independence movement or civil war

Age: 10 to adult

Concepts:
- People can have multiple perspectives on the same events

- People fighting on the same side of a conflict can have different interests

- Ethnicity, gender and economic position affect one's viewpoint

Strategies:
- Historian's Simulation Workshop

- Dramatic Arts

- Group Experience Writing

Resources: Select readings describing living conditions of each group represented in the simulation. These may come from a variety of sources, including primary sources, texts, historical fiction and biography. See bibliography for sources on different ethnic and economic groups of men and women during the Chinese and American revolutions.

Activity Profile: The Historian's Simulation Workshop is an experiential way to investigate the outlook and actions of different ethnic and economic groups of men and women in a time of conflict. In this form of simulation, students do not simply re-enact events they already know happened. Instead they are actively involved in creating the outcome. They consider what they might have thought and done had they been a member of a particular group during an historical crisis and they forge alliances with other groups in the classroom.

We provide two sample simulations—one on the Chinese Revolution and one on the American Revolution—so that you can see how to develop simulations tailored to your own curriculum. The simulations follow the same procedure, but they start with different Situation Cards. After reading the Situation Card, students are divided into various social groups present at the time of the conflict. They read historical information about the economic, political and social conditions of their group. Then they are asked to make decisions for their group—whether or not to fight in the revolution, on which side to fight, and with whom to ally. To help them decide, they develop questions to determine if other groups really have their interests at heart and can be trusted as allies. After making a final decision, the whole class together writes a history of what happened in the classroom (group experience writing) and compares it to actual historical evidence.

STEPS

Step 1. Dramatically introduce the crisis to the class by reading the Situation Card. This catapults students back to the eve of the revolution, as if they were there. (A Situation Card can be developed for any war or conflict.)

Americans in the Revolution
Situation Card

Time: 1775

Place: American colonies

Situation: Insurrection is in the air! Rumors are circulating that people are arming themselves and gathering supplies of ammunition to fight the British. The rebels say we are fighting for **FREEDOM**. . . that all men are equal and no one has the right to tell us what to do.

Neighbors are demanding to know, "Which side are you on?" Some say soldiers will be coming soon to get us to join the fight!

Is this **MY** battle?

```
┌─────────────────────────────────────────────────────────────┐
│                    Civil War in China                       │
│                    Situation Card                           │
│  Time: 1947                                                 │
│  Place: China                                               │
│  Situation: The Japanese army has surrendered! Civil War between │
│  the Kuomintang and the Chinese Communists is raging! All sides │
│  say they are fighting for FREEDOM. Some say the Communist  │
│  People's Army is declaring "Land to the Tiller!" under the Draft │
│  Agrarian Law. Debts will be canceled, the rights of landlords abol- │
│  ished and land given to those who work it. The landlords must │
│  give up their land—worth over $20 billion dollars—without com- │
│  pensation! As the military offensives sweep through the country, │
│  peasants and workers are rising up. Neighbors are demanding to │
│  know, "Which side are you on?"(25)                         │
└─────────────────────────────────────────────────────────────┘
```

Step 2. Divide students up into various groups in society during the revolutionary period in each country (approximately 3-5 students in a group). Include the following groups:

American Colonies	China
women	women
Native Americans (can be subdivided by tribe)	poor peasants
slaves	hired laborers
indentured servants	middle peasants
small farmers and craftspeople	landlords
southern plantation owners	urban merchants
northern merchants	professionals
	students

Note: In reality, these groups are not homogeneous. They may include many different people. For example, the Native American group includes many different tribes. Group membership may also be overlapping. Women, for example, belong to every group. The women's group may include women of different economic classes as well as ethnicities. The readings provided to the groups should reflect diversity as much as possible. You may add groups or subdivide the groups.

Step 3. Tell the groups that they need to define their group goals, and decide whether or not they are willing to risk their lives to fight in this war. In order to make this decision, they will need to read the materials provided for their group. From the information in the readings, each group will discuss the questions below and be ready to share responses with the class.

1. If our group were to fight to make our lives better, what are the things we would want most? What is worth risking our lives for?
2. What does "freedom" mean to our group? What kinds of freedoms do we have? What freedoms do we want?

Step 4. Tell students: The other groups in the classroom are your potential allies or foes. You need to find out where they stand on the issues you care most about. With your group, prepare at least 2 questions to ask one other group. (Time permitting, you may also prepare additional questions to ask other groups.) These questions should help you figure out what other groups really think, how they see you, and whether it is in your interest to forge alliances with them. Do they want the same things you do? Will they stand by you or betray you? Can they help you achieve your goals even if you disagree with them on some matters?

For example, in the American Revolution, the slaves might ask the northern merchants whether they will be freed if they fight on the patriot side and whether merchants in the north will give them jobs when the war is over. The women might ask the land-owning groups whether women will be free to own land in their own name when the colonies are free. The Native Americans might want to know which side will respect their land and way of life. Plantation owners might want to know if they are allying with people who have promised to free their slaves.

Step 5. After all groups have prepared questions, bring all groups together. Each group should represent itself with a large group sign. Each group in turn gets a chance to ask its questions and receive a response. In responding to a question, students can confer with their other group members. Allow time for dialogue between the groups, since questions may need follow-up and various group members may want to express their views.

Step 6. Decide whose side you're on! After all groups have had a chance to ask questions, allow each group to meet separately. Based on what they've heard, they decide:

– with whom will we ally and why?
– will we fight and why?

Each group reports its decision and gives reasons for it.

Step 7: Processing the Simulation.

• Option 1: *Group Experience Writing.* Based on the simulation, students together write their history of the revolution from multiple perspectives. The whole class synthesizes and summarizes what happened in class. To begin, ask the class the questions below, as you record their responses on a mind map:

>   – What happened in our simulation? What was it about?
>   – What did the various groups want? How did they see things differently?
>   – What happened in the end?

Then the group members organize and number their thoughts as they prepare to write an essay from the mind map.

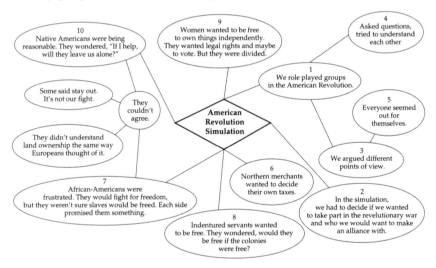

Option 2: *Complete Sentence Stems.* Another way to process the simulation is to allow students to discuss the thoughts, feelings and questions they are left with. To help, they might individually complete sentence stems:

>   – I think…
>   – I feel…
>   – I wonder…
>   – What would have happened if…?

Then, compare what happened in the simulation to what really happened in history. Ask students if they think anything happened in the simulation that never actually happened in history. They may be surprised to learn, for example, that indeed colonial women did raise issues of women's rights 150 years before they got the vote; or that an African-Seminole alliance fought the U.S. army in Florida's early history; or that among the Patriots, conflicts between wealthy people and landless or land poor people broke out even in the midst of the war; or that many African-Americans were heroes in the Revolutionary War.

Ask students why they think these stories are not familiar to us. What questions does this simulation raise that they'd like to research? You may ask them to reread chapters of their textbooks and note places in the text where they think another voice needs to be heard.

CURRENT CONFLICTS

Activity #3

THE SPIRITS AT CASTLELAKE BEACH:
CHILDREN'S PERSPECTIVES ON THE ENVIRONMENT

Topic: Effects of development on the natural world

Age: 10 to adult

Concepts:
- Land use and rights of indigenous peoples
- Conservation of natural resources
- Civic action

Strategy:
- Creating Art: Imagine and Draw

Resources:
- L. Temple, (Ed.) *Dear World: How Children Around the World Feel about Our Environment* (this is a collection of photographs, drawings and letters of children around the world expressing their concerns about nature and pollution)
- Newspaper or magazine articles which highlight global or local environmental issues

Activity Profile: Children around the world are worried about the environment they will inherit. They are concerned about clear cutting in forests, deforestation, acid rain, oil spills, radiation, air pollution, water pollution, noise pollution and the effects of war on nature. In this activity, the teacher reads an article or letter in which a child voices concern about a special place in nature. Students imagine what that place looks like and what the place *would* look like if further development were to occur. They draw two pictures, a Before and After. Through the process of imagining and drawing, they express their perceptions in two contrasting scenes. They use the two drawings as starting points for identifying what special meaning places have to various groups of people.

Background: Peoples around the world have different relationships to the land and different concepts of land ownership. The natural world often has meanings for indigenous peoples connected to spirituality as well as daily life, and indeed there may be an integral connection between the two. Navajo place-names, for example, may reflect moral stories which young people hear from their elders. In ancient Hawaii, land belonged to the gods and could not be owned by people. Ruling chiefs, as descendants of the gods, governed the use of lands. Today, ecology and conservation movements often align with indigenous peoples in their search for support to preserve land and natural resources. In 1995, Canadian tribal chiefs, for instance, sought support for blocking clear cutting logging on ancestral lands. In rain forest areas of the world, native peoples have lived for thousands of years, using the forest in a sustainable manner. Today, the destruction of the rain forest affects the health of the whole planet. Those working to conserve natural environments are often pitted against those promoting economic development. Researching environmental issues from diverse perspectives can help students form and articulate their own values.

STEPS

Step 1. Students have colored pens, crayons or colored pencils on their desks. They have folded a piece of drawing paper in half. Tell them that they will be doing two drawings: a "Before" and an "After" drawing. To do these drawings they will *first listen , then imagine and last, draw.* There is a special place that they will be thinking about. Someone is worried about this place because of a change that might happen to it.

118

Step 2. Read a short sentence which will identify the place in nature and the worry.

. . . .

"I am worried about the mining at Castlelake Beach on Melville Island."

— from *Dear World*

"I'm worried about what will happen to _____ when _____."

— from a local newspaper

. . . .

Step 3. Identify a passage in the reading that describes the beauty or value of the natural habitat to the author. Read the passage(s) to the students. Ask them to close their eyes and imagine the place as it is now. Ask them to picture in their minds the beach, the island, the trees, the water (or whatever features or details would help them see the place in their mind's eye). Ask them to imagine with their senses (see, hear, smell, touch) what this place is like. What do they see there? What sounds do they hear? What scents? What textures are there on the sand, trees, plants, water? Allow time for them to imagine. When it seems appropriate, ask them to open their eyes, pick up their crayons or pencils and draw this place. Often it is helpful to draw in silence, as this helps students to continue to access their own individual images.

Step 4. Ask students to share drawings with a partner, comparing the details of what they have put in their pictures. Note the similarities and differences in the drawings.

Step 5. Identify and read a passage that expresses the writer's worry and describes what could happen to the environment. Ask students what in their picture would be different if these changes occurred. Ask them to draw the second picture to show these changes.

Jesse Reiter-Skolnick

In the example from *Dear World*, Dianne Moore is worried about her place because she is afraid that the digging will disturb the spirits of her relatives who are buried there.

> I am worried about the mining at Castlelake Beach on Melville Island because my grandfather and other relatives have been buried there and they will disturb the spirits. If they mine Castlelake they will dig out all the trees and make a big hole in the ground and when the tide comes in it will fill the hole and cover up the graves."
>
> Your friend Dianne Moore, age 9[26]

Step 6. Post drawings on the board, allowing students time to look at all of them.

Discuss: What did you notice in the drawings? What similarities did you see among the "Before" drawings? What similarities did you see in the "After" drawings? What differences did you see between the "Before" and "After" pictures?

Step 7. Now help students focus on perspectives. Discuss the following questions:

– *From what you heard in the reading, what do you know about the people who say they are worried?*
– *Who are they?*
– *Why is the place particularly meaningful to them?*
– *Who might not understand the meaning of the place to them? Why?*

Make a list of people who should see the drawings in order to better understand. What else do they need to know? What else do we need to know?

Step 8. (optional) Now have students use additional resources to research further the proposed changes. Using their notes and their drawings, they could:

1. write a text to explain their drawings, creating a school exhibit
2. prepare arguments that support the project or support those who want to stop it.
3. write letters to local officials, or
4. practice voicing their views in the classroom in preparation for an actual visit to the board or community meeting.

Activity #4

NEWCOMERS IN OUR TOWN: A DIALOGUE POEM

Topic:	Stereotypes of immigrants, minorities or the poor; current events; local history
Age:	10 and up
Concepts:	• More than one perspective on the same event • Difficulties faced by newcomers to a community • Backlash against immigrants
Strategy:	Writing: Dialogue Poems
Resources:	• News articles • Other possible sources: children's literature, primary sources, texts • Sample dialogue poem (included)

Activity Profile: Students can create and dramatically read dialogue poems to explore different views of the same events. In a dialogue poem, two characters speak about a common experience or event from two different perspectives. The perspectives are often in opposition to one another. The poem contains several "common lines," which anchor the poem and convey something that is shared. Common lines are placed dramatically at key points in the poem and read simultaneously when the poem is performed. The poem is written and performed in dual voices, powerfully showing how differently we can feel about the same event. In the process of writing a dialogue poem, students really have to think about what could be different about two people's (or groups') experience. It may not have previously occurred to them that there *could* be several views of a "factual" news event.

Many topics, historical and contemporary, lend themselves to the writing of dialogue poems. Upper elementary and secondary students can create powerful poems when given concrete sources to read. Information can be provided by newspaper or magazine articles on controversial topics (immigration, war, local disputes, welfare, protests). Fiction, texts or primary sources (diaries, journals, etc.) may also be used.

Background: The following poem was created from a local newspaper article about farm workers facing poverty and moving to cities. It told the story of Ramon's family, one of many immigrant families, who are moving from croplands to suburban towns as the farm work dwindles. The article describes one community's reaction to fast growing immigrant neighborhoods in their town.

STEPS

Step 1. Select a news article on a controversial topic or event. In this case, we used a current news article about immigrant workers in a suburban community. (Alternatively, you might choose to use an historical event you have been studying.)

Step 2. Read the piece out loud, distributing copies to students.

Step 3. In whole class or in small group format, have students identify groups (or persons) who might have different views of the events reported in the article. Brainstorm on the board (whole class), or on paper (in small cooperative groups) what differences might be found between the two views. Make a mind map or chart. Students will refer to these later as they write the poem.

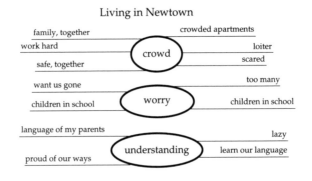

Living in Newtown

family, together		crowded apartments
work hard	crowd	loiter
safe, together		scared
want us gone		too many
children in school	worry	children in school
language of my parents		lazy
proud of our ways	understanding	learn our language

122

Step 4. Tell students they will be writing a poem that will pair two views. Tell them a dialogue poem has a common line that says something about what both groups share. It also has separate lines that describe the way each person or group sees things. With a student volunteer, read the following model poem to the class. The common line "living in Newtown" is read simultaneously by both readers. Then the readers alternate lines. Reader #1 reads "is new to us"; Reader #2 reads "is not what it used to be" followed by Reader #1 "we are crowded..." etc. until you again reach the common line to be read together. Ask students to identify the common line and the separate lines.

LIVING IN Newtown

LIVING IN Newtown	LIVING IN Newtown
is new to us	
	is not what it used to be
We are crowded but my family can be together	
	They crowd into apartments on my block.
Each morning I look for jobs scrubbing floors, doing yard work so my children won't go hungry	
	They loiter at the corner and I am scared to walk by.
I work long, hard hours	
	Why do they stand there? Why don't they work?
I AM WORRIED	I AM WORRIED
Because some around us want us gone	
	Because too many of them are moving in
They say my children can't go to school	
	They say their children will go to school with mine. I pay taxes so MY children can go to school

I do work they don't want to do, for little pay. They need my work	
	What do they contribute?
I DON'T UNDERSTAND THEM	I DON'T UNDERSTAND THEIR LANGUAGE They are too lazy to learn our language and our ways
I am proud of mine....I am learning theirs	
I speak the language of my parents	
I am proud my children will learn our ways...and new ways	
	I don't feel safe anymore
Here we will make a new start My family will feel safe	
LIVING IN NEWTOWN	LIVING IN NEWTOWN

Step 5. Brainstorm ideas for common poem lines from the news article with which students will work.

Step 6. Referring to their mind maps, have students draft the poem in small groups or pairs.

Step 7. Ask students to rehearse and read their poems dramatically to the class.

Step 8. To process the activity, ask students why they think people would see things so differently. What fears, hopes, economic demands, previous ideas, prejudices, stereotypes might come into play? What does one group see that the other does not? What might help these two groups see each other's point of view? Then ask students what they learned from writing the poem. What more they would want to know? Generate questions for further research.

Activity #5

OWLS AND JOBS

Topic:	Loggers and environmentalists: controversy over the habitat of the "spotted owl"
Age:	10 and up

124

Concepts:	• Different perspectives on commercial use of resources and environmental protection
	• Responsibility and stewardship for natural resources
	• Land use and rights of indigenous peoples
Strategies:	• Creating Art: Imagine and Draw
	• Dramatic Arts
Resources:	• Newspaper or magazine articles which highlight an environmental controversy (this activity uses the example of the habitat of the spotted owl)
	• Children's books related to this topic.

Activity Profile: This activity can be done with any environmental issue where there is tension between commercial use of resources and environmental protection. Students use imaginative drawings to explore diverse views. In this example students draw different perspectives of people who live near a redwood forest in a logging area. After looking at photographs of the forest, sensory images and personal experiences are recorded on a class mind map. Next students read individual profiles of various people in the community and draw what the forest means to these people. They then create a local television program in which the community hears these individuals talk about their views of the forest.

Background: Around the world, logging threatens to destroy sacred sites of native peoples, or to interfere with their hunting, fishing and ways of life. In this example, the controversy over the northern spotted owl, designated as a threatened species in 1990, highlights the diversity of perspectives on land use and ecology. The spotted owl is an "indicator species," a species that gives early warning signals of damage to the ecosystem. Spotted owls, thus, can tell us whether our ancient forests are disappearing too quickly. The spotted owl habitat in British Columbia, Canada, and the Northwest Coast of the United States is old-growth and mixed old-growth and mature forest. In 1990, the Endangered Species Act, a rigorous piece of United States environmental legislation, declared "old-growth" forests off-limits to the timber industry. The controversy that ensued, and continues, calls into question practices like "clear-cutting," in which whole areas of forest are cleared. It also raises the issue of whether the need for jobs and the need for environmental protection need to be in opposition.

Step 1. Show one or more pictures of the forest or land area you choose for your activity (in this case, the redwood forest). Ask students to imagine that they are in the picture. Ask questions like:

What do you see? What do you hear? What is on the ground beneath your feet? How does it feel as you walk on the pathway? What do you notice about the trees? What is the bark like? How many different groups of small redwoods do you see encircling the tall ones? How are they growing? How tall are the trees? What do you see when you look up? What animals do you see? What insects do you see and hear? What flowers are growing in the forest? What light and shadows patterns are there? What do you see that is moving? What do you see that is still?

At the end of this questioning period, ask students to once again imagine they are in the forest and to appreciate being there. The purpose of this is to provide ample time for the sensory experience before moving on.

Step 2. Next, ask students what forests mean to them in their own lives. Construct a group mind map, with students giving ideas as you record what they say. Your mind map can have categories like those below or may simply reflect student comments.

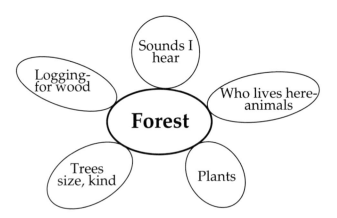

Step 3. Now that students have explored their own relation to the forest, they are ready to think about how different views of a natural resource can create controversy.

Setting the scene

Tell the students that people appreciate the forest in diverse ways, as they can see from the mind map of their ideas. People use the forest for work, for recreation, for survival; people appreciate its beauty. In one town, people's different views caused many arguments. Old-growth forests became the center of a controversy. They were the home of the northern spotted owl, a threatened species. Some people said that the forests were their tribal lands, important as sacred sites, and as places where their traditional ways of life can be maintained. Other people worried about their jobs in logging; they felt that jobs were more important than maintaining old ways or preserving owls. Other people said that the way forests were being cut down destroyed a resource that could never be replaced. Some loggers thought that different ways of cutting the forests were possible. There were protests, billboards, town meetings and arguments as neighbors and people from outside the area came to voice their views.

Step 4. Each student is going to be one of the people in the town. Assign Redwoods Cards (below) for students to read, individually or in small groups. Each card contains information about a different person who lives in the town.

Redwoods Cards

You are: James Gilroy, a third generation logger. You support your wife and three children by working for a lumber company. It is the only job you have ever had.

You are: Jack Smith, a seventy-year-old "old-timer." You have hunted in the forest and fished in the river that runs through it all your life. You built the house you live in now with your two sons, Jack Jr. and Jackson. Hunting and fishing have always been an important part of your family life. You are friends with people of the Nuxalk tribe, and your families share hunting and fishing areas of the forest.

You are: a chief of the Nuxalk tribe. Your tribe hunts and fishes on this land and you are a leader in maintaining the old ways and traditions of your people. A few years ago, you spent two weeks in jail because you protested and blockaded a logging road that was going into an area of old growth timber.

You are: Steve Rush, the owner of Rush Lumber, a small independent lumber mill. You started out with twenty employees, but because of the declaration of the spotted owl being an endangered species, seven million acres of land were declared off limits to loggers. You have had to lay off some workers.

You are: Louise Turner, a fifty-year-old furniture store owner, whose grandfather has passed down the business to you. You rely on the local lumber yard and saw mill for wood for your furniture. You ship your unusual furniture to many large cities across the state. You have had to decrease your production rate due to the lack of lumber.

You are: Lisa Valdez. You grew up in this area and have always loved the forest. When you were in college, you started studying the spotted owl, and you have noticed that in the past ten years since you started research in this area, that their numbers have declined. You think it is because of the logging. You have been studying the alliances of environmental groups with tribal peoples, and you are organizing a meeting for different groups that have forest preservation high on their list of priorities.

Note: If you are using another issue, you may want to make up cards by brainstorming points of view with students. Students can participate in creating the people who would have different views, or they may be actual people they've read about.

Step 5. As the person in the card, the student considers:

– *What does the forest mean to me?*
– *What worries do I have?*
– *What do changes in the forest mean to me?*

Tell each student to draw the answers to these questions. What would need to go into the picture?

Here are three examples drawn by a 9-year-old, 11-year-old, and a 5-year-old.

Louise Turner

by ALEX Boyer

Steve Rush

BY Elizabeth DeLoen Boyer

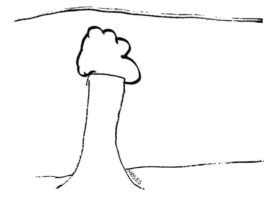

Step 6. Post drawings on the board, grouping them by persons represented. Allow time for students to look carefully at the details of the drawings. Discuss differences in the pictures. Help students to identify why there are different perspectives here, and why the drawings show different things.

– *Why is the forest important to_____?*
– *What policy does _____ support?*
– *What does or would this mean to that person's life?*

Step 7. (optional) Have students volunteer to represent each person in dramatizing a panel discussion on a news program exploring the issue. The "studio audience" can prepare questions for the panel. Give students time to gather information and prepare questions.

....

REFERENCES

PART ONE

1. Adapted from Schriver, Anita *Look at Us: Our Stories Connect Us.* Oakland, CA: Bancroft Middle School (1993). A project of the Bancroft Middle School Human Relations Club.

2. The Commission on Minority Participation in Education and American Life. (May, 1988). *One-Third of a Nation.* Washington, D.C.: The American Council On Education.

    U.N. report cited in McLeod, R.G. "Human Migration Enters New Era." In San Francisco Chronicle, August 9, 1994, p.1.

    Canadian statistics quoted in Christensen, C.P. "Cross-Cultural Awareness: A Development Process in a Multicultural and Multiracial Society." In Multiculturalism/Interculturalisme, vol. XVI. no 1 (1995); Snyder, T. Youth Indicators 1996. Washington, D.C.: National Center for Educational Statistics.

    Greene, Maxine. *The Dialectic of Freedom.* New York: Teachers College Press, 1988.

3. Freedman, Russell. Cited in Tunnel, Michael O. and Ammon, Richard. "The Story of Ourselves: Fostering Multiple Historical Perspectives." *Social Education,* Vol. 60, no. 4 (1996), pp. 212-215.

4. Levstik, Linda. "Any History Is Someone's History: Listening to Multiple Voices from the Past." *Social Education,* Vol 61, no. 1 (1997), pp. 48-52.

5. Dulberg, Nancy. *Perspective-Taking and Empathy in History and Social Studies: A Study of Fifth Grade Students' Thinking.* Doctoral Dissertation, University of California at Berkeley. 1998.

    Downey, Matthew. "Perspective-Taking and Historical Thinking: Doing History in a Fifth Grade Classroom." Paper presented at the annual meeting of the American Education Research Association. S.F., (April, 1995).

6. DeVries, Rheta and Zan, Betty, *Moral Classrooms, Moral Children: Creating a Constructivist Atmosphere in Early Education.* New York: Teachers College Press, 1994, p. 2.

7. Levstik, Linda. "Teaching History: A Definitional and Developmental Dilemma." In Atwood, V.A. (Ed.). *Elementary School Social Studies: Research As a Guide to Practice.* Washington, D.C.: National Council for the Social Studies, 1986.

    Shemilt, Denis *Schools Council History 13-16 Project: Evaluation Study.* Edinburgh: Holmes, McDougall, 1980.

    Downey, Matthew. "Perspective-Taking and Historical Thinking: Doing History in a Fifth Grade Classroom." Paper presented at the annual meeting of the American Education Research Association, S.F., (April 1995).

8. Yee, Sylvia & Kokin, Lisa. *Got Me A Story To Tell.* San Francisco, CA: St. John's Educational Threshold Center, 1977.

9. Banks, James. "Reducing Prejudice in Children: Guidelines From Research." *Social Studies and the Young Learner.* Vol. 5, no. 2 (1992-93) p. 5.

Derman–Sparks, Louise and the A.B.C. Task Force. *Anti-Bias Curriculum: Tools for Empowering Young Children.* Washington, D.C.: National Association for the Education of Young Children, 1989.

10. Derman-Sparks, 1989, p. 4.

11. Pate, Glen. "Research On Reducing Prejudice." *Social Education,* Vol. 52, no. 4 (1988), p. 287.

Gabelko, Nina Hersch. "Prejudice Reduction In Secondary Schools." *Social Education.* Vol. 52, no. 4 (1988), pp. 276-279.

12. Cohen, Elizabeth. "Restructuring the Classroom: Conditions For Productive Small Groups." *Review of Educational Research.* Vol. 64, no. 1 (1994), pp. 1-35.

13. Arrien, Angeles. *Signs of Life.* Sonoma, CA: Arcus Publishing Company, 1992.

14. Piaget, Jean. *The Construction of Reality in the Child.* New York: Basic Books, 1954.

Piaget, Jean. *Intelligence and Affectivity: The Relation During Child Development.* Palo Alto, California: Annual Reviews, 1954/ 1981.

Bruner, Jerome. *The Process of Education.* Cambridge: Harvard University Press, 1960.

McCarthy, Bernice. *The 4MAT System: Teaching to Learning Styles with Right/ Left Mode Techniques.* Barrington, IL: Excel, Inc., 1987.

15. Dewey, John. *The Child and the Curriculum. The School and Society.* University of Chicago Press, 1960.

Dewey, John. *Interest and Effort in Education.* Edwardsville, Illinois: Southern Illinois Press, 1975.

16. West, Jan (Ed.) *The Immigrant Experience, Vol. 2: Teaching with Primary Sources Series.* Petersborough, NH: Cobblestone Publishing, Inc., 1996.

17. Selected by Katz, Jacqueline & William Katz, *Making Our Way: America at the Turn of the Century in the Words of the Poor and Powerless.* New York: Dial Press, 1975 p. 196.

18. Katz & Katz, *Making Our Way.* 1976. pp. 189-192.

19. Nancy Flowers, "Human Rights Education and the Arts: An Introduction," Amnesty International, winter 1996, p. 2 (vol 7, no. 1).

20. Littlechild, George. *This Land is My Land,* Emeryville, CA: Children's Book Press, 1993, p. 20.

21. Mason, Kathy. *Going Beyond Words.* Tucson, AZ: Zephyr Press, 1991.

22. Cowell, Juliette. Unpublished manuscript. *Mapping Insights: A Graphic Process for Generating and Organizing Ideas,* by Cynthia Alexander, Juliette Cowell, Theodora Maestre, and Nancy Zimmerman, 1983.

REFERENCES

PART TWO

1. Meltzer, Milton, *Cheap Raw Material: How Our Youngest Workers are Exploited and Abused.* New York: Viking, 1994, pp. 37-38.
2. Kay Taus cited in Louise Derman-Sparks, *Anti-Bias Curriculum.* Washington, D.C.: National Association for the Education of Young Children, 1989, p. 146.
3. Flournoy, Valerie, *The Patchwork Quilt.* New York: Scholastic (1996).
4. Fassler, D. and K. Danforth, *Coming to America: The Kid's Book about Immigration.* Burlington, Vermont: Waterfront Books, 1993.
5. McLeod, Ramon G. *"Human Migration Enters A New Era."* San Francisco Chronicle, August 9, 1994.
6. Wilkes, Sybella. *One Day We Had To Run!* Brookfield, Connecticut: Millbrook Press, 1994, p. 58.
7. Gillett, Paula. "Cambodian Refugees: An Introduction to Their History and Culture" in Karen Jorgensen-Esmaili *New Faces of Liberty: A Curriculum for Teaching About Today's Refugees, and Immigrants, Grades 5-8.* Zellerach Family Fund: Berkeley, California, 1988.
8. Wilkes, Sybella. *One Day We Had To Run!* p. 7.
9. Bernard's story is retold by Rae Reiter.
10. Wilkes, Sybella. *One Day We Had To Run!* p. 75.
11. Yee, S. & L. Kokin. *Got Me A Story To Tell.* San Francisco, California: St. John's Educational Threshold Center, 1977.
12. Cherokee tribal members in a letter to John Ross, principal chief of the Cherokees. Cited in Fremon, D.K. (1994). *The Trail of Tears.* New York: New Discovery Books (Macmillan).
13. John Burnett, 2nd Brigade, Mounted Infantry, "Removal of the Cherokees, 1838-39", p. 2, in Cherokee Legends and the Trail of Tears, adapted by Thomas Underwood from the 19th annual report of the Bureau of American Ethnology, 1956, McLemore Printing, Tenn. Cited in Grame, Ritu, (1995) *Trail of Tears: Cherokee Nation Forced From Native Lands.*
14. Rebecca Neugin, *Memories of the Trail,* quoted in Richard Thornton, *American Indian Holocaust and Survival* (Norman, Oklahoma: University of Oklahoma Pewaa, 1987), p. 117. Cited in Fremon, D.K. (1994). *The Trail of Tears.* New York: New Discovery Books (Macmillan) p. 9.
15. Cherokee Tribe, Memorial sent to the United States government, quoted in Van Every, Dale, *Disinherited: The Lost Birthright of the American Indian* (New York: William Morrow, 1966), p. 15. Cited in Fremon, D.K. (1994). *The Trail of Tears.* New York: New Discovery Books (Macmillan) p. 90

16. Cherokee Chief John Ross, in Van Every, p. 99. Cited in Fremon, D.K. (1994). *The Trail of Tears*. New York: New Discovery Books (Macmillan) p. 40

17. Crockett, Davy, (1992) *Davy Crockett's Own Story as Written by Himself: The Autobiography of America's Great Folk Hero*. Stamford, CT: Longmeadow Press, pp. 155-157.

18. President Martin Van Buren, quoted in Gloria Jahoda, *The Trail of Tears: The Story of the American Indian Removals 1813-1855* (New York: Holt, Reinhard and Winston, 1975) p. 230. *The Trail of Tears*. New York: New Discovery Books (Macmillan) p. 74.

19. Georgia volunteer soldier, quoted in Thorton, p. 116. Cited in Fremon, D.K. (1994). *The Trail of Tears*. New York: New Discovery Books (Macmillan) p. 81.

20. Thomas Jefferson, quoted in Van Every, p. 89. Cited in Fremon, D.K. (1994). *The Trail of Tears*. New York: New Discovery Books (Macmillan) p. 22.

21. Georgia State Legislature, quoted in Carter III, Samul, Cherokee Sunset: A Nation Betrayed (Garden City, New York: Doubleday, 1976), p. 73. Cited in Fremon, p. 43.

22. Chief Justice Marshall and the Governor of Georgia, respectively, quoted in Carter, p. 131. Cited in Fremon, D.K. (1994). *The Trail of Tears*. New York: New Discovery Books (Macmillan) pp. 59-60.

23. Gail Sadalla, Meg Holmberg, and Jim Halligan. *Conflict Resolution: An Elementary Curriculum*. San Francisco, California: The Community Board Program, Inc., 1990, p. 1-2.

24. Sadalla et. al., *Conflict Resolution* p. 1-2.

25. Hinton, William, *Fanshen: A Documentary of Revolution in a Chinese Village*. New York: Vintage Books, 1968.

26. Temple, Lannis (ed.), *Dear World: How Children Around the World Feel About Our Environment*. New York: Random House, 1993, p. 75.

....

TEACHER RESOURCE

BIBLIOGRAPHIES

FOR ACTIVITIES CHAPTERS

CHAPTER 4: THROUGH OUR MEMORIES

Bartone, E. *Peppe the Lamplighter.* New York: Lee & Shepard Books, 1993
Friedman, I. *How My Parents Learned to Eat.* Boston: Houghton Mifflin, 1984
Havill, J. *Treasure Nap.* Boston: Houghton Mifflin, 1992
Hendershot, J. *In Coal Country.* New York: Alfred A. Knopf, 1987
Littlechild, G. *This Land is My Land.* Emeryville, California: Children's Book Press, 1993
Oberman, S. *The Always Prayer Shawl.* Honesdale, Pennsylvania: Boyds Mills Press, 1994
Polacco, P. *The Keeping Quilt.* New York: Simon & Schuster, 1988
Ringgold, F. *Tar Beach.* New York: Crown Publishers, 1991
Rylant, C. *When I Was Young in the Mountains.* New York: E.P. Dutton, 1982
Say, A. *Grandfather's Journey.* Boston: Houghton Mifflin, 1993
Yarbrough, C. *Cornrows.* New York: Coward-McCann, 1979
Weitzman, D. *My Backyard History Book.* Boston: Little Brown and Co., 1975
Wheatley, N. and Rawlins D. *My Place.* Adelaide, Australia: Australia In Print Inc., 1989
Zolotow, C. *The Sky Was Blue.* New York: Harper & Row, 1963

CHAPTER 5: THROUGH OUR WORK

Baylor, B. *The Table Where Rich People Sit.* New York: Charles Scribner's Sons, 1994
Blumberg, R. *Full Steam Ahead: The Race to Build a Transcontinental Railroad.* Washington, D.C.: National Geographic Society, 1996
Castaneda, O. *Abuela's Weave.* New York: Lee & Low, 1993
Coerr, E. *The Josefina Story Quilt.* New York: Harper Trophy, 1986
D'Aluisio, F. & P. Menzel. *Women in the Material World.* San Francisco: Sierra Club Books, 1996
Flournoy, V. *The Patchwork Quilt.* New York: Dial Books, 1985
Freedman, R. *Kids at Work: Lewis Hine and the Crusade Against Child Labor.* New York: Clarion Books, 1994
Guback, Georgia. *Luka's Quilt.* New York: Greenwillow Books, 1994
Johnston, T. & DePaola, T. *The Quilt Story.* New York: G. Putnam Sons, 1985
Kinsey–Warnock, N. *The Canada Geese Quilt.* New York: Cobblehill/Dutton, 1989
Lesis, A.A. *The Mountain Artisans Quilting Book.* New York: Macmillan, 1973

Meltzer, Milton. *Cheap Raw Material: How Our Youngest Workers Are Exploited and Abused*. New York: Viking, 1994

Menzel, P. *Material World: A Global Family Portrait*. San Francisco, California: Sierra Club Books, 1994

Parton, D. *Coat of Many Colors*. New York: HarperCollins, 1994.

Paterson, K. *Lyddie*. New York: Lodestar Books, 1991

Polacco, P. *The Keeping Quilt*. New York: Simon & Schuster, 1988

Takaki, R. *Journey to Gold Mountain: The Chinese in Nineteenth Century America*. New York: Chelsea House, 1994

Yep, L. *Dragon's Gate*. New York: Scholastic, Inc., 1993.

Williams, V.B. *A Chair for My Mother*. New York: Greenwillow Books, 1982

CHAPTER 6: THROUGH OUR MIGRATIONS

Altman, L.J. *Amelia's Road*. New York: Lee & Low Books Inc., 1993

Atkin, S.B. *Voices From the Fields: Children of Migrant Farmworkers Tell Their Stories*. Boston: Little, Brown and Company, 1993

Cohen, B. *Molly's Pilgrim*. New York: Bantam Skylark, 1983

Coles, R. *Uprooted Children: The Early Life of Migrant Farm Workers*. Pittsburgh: University of Pittsburgh Press, 1970

Dorros, A. *Radio Man: A Story in English and Spanish*. New York: HarperCollins, 1993

Fassler, D. and Danforth, K. *Coming To America: The Kids' Book About Immigration*. Burlington, Vermont: Waterfront Books, 1993

Gillett, P. "Cambodian Refugees: An Introduction to their History and Culture, in Jorgensen–Esmaili, K. *New Faces of Liberty: A Curriculum for Teaching about Today's Refugees and Immigrants, Grades 5 through 8*. Berkeley, CA: Zellerbach Family Fund, 1988

Knight, M.B. *Who Belongs Here? An American Story*. Gardiner, Maine: Tilbury House, 1993

Kurelek, W. *They Sought a New World: The Story of European Immigration to North America*. Montreal: Tundra Books, 1985

Lawrence, J. *The Great Migration: An American Story*. New York: HarperCollins, 1993

Paek, Min. *Aekyung's Dream*. San Francisco, CA: Children's Book Press, 1988

Shea, P.D. *The Whispering Cloth: A Refugee's Story*. Honesdale, Pennsylvania: Boyds Mills Press, 1995.

Wilkes, Sybella. *One Day We Had To Run!* Brookfield, CT: Millbrook Press, 1994.

Yee, S. & L. Kokin. *Got Me a Story to Tell*. San Francisco, CA: St. John's Educational Threshold Center, 1977

CHAPTER 7: THROUGH CONFLICT AND CHANGE

Baker, J. *Where the Forest Meets the Sea*. New York: Scholastic, Inc., 1987

Brimner, L.D. *Voices From the Camps: Internment of Japanese Americans During World War II*. Toronto: Franklin Watts, 1994

Conrat, M. & R. *Executive Order 9066: The Internment of 110,000 Japanese Americans*. University of California, Los Angeles: Asian American Studies Center, 1992

Craighead–George, Jean. *There's an Owl in the Shower*. New York: Scholastic Books, 1995

Davis, Burke. *Black Heroes of the American Revolution*. New York: Harcourt Brace Jovanovich, Publishers, 1976

DePauw, Linda Grant. *Founding Mothers: Women of America in the Revolutionary Era*. Boston, MA: Houghton Mifflin, 1975

Filipovic, Z. *Zlata's Diary*. New York: Viking, 1994

Fremon, D. *The Trail of Tears*. New York: New Discovery Books.

Gates, Henry Louis Jr., (Ed.) *The Classic Slave Narratives* and *Six Women's Slave Narratives*. New York: Penguin, 1987

Hinton, William. *Fanshen: A Documentary of Revolution in a Chinese Village*. New York: Vintage Books, 1968

Hoobler, D. and Hoobler, T. *The Trail On Which They Wept: The Story of a Cherokee Girl*. Morristown, New Jersey: Silver Burdett Press, 1992

Hoestlandt, J. *Star of Fear, Star of Hope*. New York: Walker, 1995

Katz, W.L. *Black Indians: A Hidden Heritage*. New York: Atheneum, 1986

Keister, D. *Fernando's Gift; El Regalo de Fernando*. San Francisco: The Sierra Club 1995

Lester, Julius. *To Be a Slave*. New York: Scholastic, 1968

Lowry, L. *Number the Stars*. Boston: Houghton–Mifflin, 1989

Meltzer, M. (Ed.) *In Their Own Words: A History of the American Negro*. New York: Crowell, 1964-67

Monk, L. (Ed.) *Ordinary Americans: U.S. History Through the Eyes of Everyday People*. Alexandria, VA.: Close-Up Publishing, 1994

Pettit, J. *A Time To Fight Back: True Stories of Wartime Resistance*. Boston: Houghton Mifflin, 1996

Polacco, P. *Pink and Say*. New York: Philomel Books, 1994

Rocha, R. and Roth, O. *The Universal Declaration of Human Rights: An Adaptation for Children*.

Silverstein, A. V. & R. *The Spotted Owl*. Brookfield, CT: The Millbrook Press, 1994

Sisulu, E. B. *The Day Gogo Went To Vote: South Africa, April 1994*. London: Little, Brown and Company, 1996

Tappage, M. A. & Speare, J. (Ed.) *The Big Tree and the Little Tree*. Winnipeg, Manitoba/Canada: Pemmican Publications Inc., 1986

Temple, Lannis. (Ed.) *Dear World: How Children Around the World Feel about Our Environment*. New York: Random House, 1993

Uchida, Yoshiko. *Journey to Topaz: A Story of the Japanese-American Evacuation*. New York: Scribner, 1971

Walter, Mildred Pitts. *Second Daughter: The Story of a Slave Girl*. New York: Scholastic, 1996

Wolfson, Evelyn. *The Iroquois*. Brookfield, CT: Millbrook Press, 1992

Zinn, Howard. *A People's History of the United States*. New York: Harper and Row, 1980

. . . .

GENERAL RESOURCES

FOR TEACHERS

Derman-Sparks, Louise and the A.B.C. Task Force. *Anti-Bias Curriculum: Tools for Empowering Young Children*. Washington, D.C.: National Association for the Education of Young Children, 1990

Levstik, L. & Barton, K. (1997). *Doing History: Investigating with Children in Elementary and Middle Schools*. Mahwah, NJ: Lawrence Erlbaum Associates.

Muse, Daphne (ed.) *The New Press Guide to Multicultural Resources for Young Readers*. New York: New Press, 1997 (1-56584-339-8)

National Women's History Project. Windsor, California.

International Rivers Network, 1847 Berkeley Way, CA, USA, 94703, (510) 848-1155.

Schniedewind, N. & Davidson, E. (1983). *Open Minds to Equality: A Sourcesbook of Learning Activities to Promote Race, Sex, Class and Age Equity*. Boston, Allyn and Bacon.

Teaching Tolerance, published by the Southern Poverty Law Center, Montgomery Alabama.

Social Education, Journal of the National Council for the Social Studies, Washington D.C.

Weitzman, D. (1975) *My Backyard History Book*. Canada: Little Brown and Co.